News Writing
for
Non-Professionals

News Writing
for
Non-Professionals

W. C. Line

Nelson-Hall nh **Chicago**

Library of Congress Cataloging in Publication Data

Line, W   C
  News writing for non-professionals.

  Includes Index.
  1. Publicity. 2. Press releases. I. Title.
HM263.L52   659.2   78-20771
ISBN 0-88229-348-6

10   9   8   7   6   5   4   3   2

Contents

Introduction
Chapter 1 Materials 1
The typewriter ... 1 Buying a typewriter ... 2 Typewriter maintenance
...4 Ribbons and papers ... 4 Typographical errors ... 5 Other materials
...6 Making copies ... 6 Brief review ... 7
Chapter 2 Format 9
What goes where ... 9 Slugging a story ... 10 Distribution line ... 11
Release date ... 12 Personal information ... 14 Headlines ... 15 Space for
the editor ... 15 Two more taboos ... 17 Sample format ... 18
Chapter 3 News Style 19
What is news style? ... 19 Dates and times ... 22 Polite address ... 25
Professional titles ... 27 Official titles ... 29 Military titles ... 30 Abbrevia-
tions ... 31 How to write numbers ... 32 Large numbers ... 33 Monetary
figures ... 34 Percentages ... 34 Fractions ... 35 A final word ... 35
Chapter 4 Policy 37
Raison d'être ... 37 News value ... 40 The value of space ... 43
Multiple submissions ... 44 Dugan's definition ... 44 Telephone numbers
...45 Deadlines ... 46 Letters to the editor ... 47 Pictures ... 48 Living
with policy ... 48
Chapter 5 Grammar 51
The sound of news ... 51 The passive voice ... 53 The false passive
...54 Other errors ... 55 Combining ideas ... 56 Adjectives and adverbs
...57 Direct quotations ... 57 Punctuating quotations ... 61 The third
person ... 62 The present perfect tense ... 63 Punctuation ... 64 Do not
oversimplify ... 68 Capitalization ... 69 Spelling ... 71 Hyphenated words
...72 Before going on ... 72
Chapter 6 The News Story 75
A prose form ... 75 The difficulty of simplicity ... 76 Get to the point
...76 The lead and the body ... 77 Interrogative leads ... 78 The Five W's
...79 More complex stories ... 81 Organization events ... 82 Shotgun leads
...85 Series stories ... 86 An ear for news ... 89 Negative leads ... 90

Improving the lead ...92 Reports about meetings ...97 Widening appeal ...99 The guest speaker ...100 What the fuss is about ...106

Chapter 7   The Feature Story 1 7

Your chance to be creative ...107 Modifying the news triangle ...109 Lead taboos ...114 Human interest ...114 Vicarious experience ...116 Dramatic imagery ...117 Selecting the proper image ...117 Gilding the lily ...118 Using the pun ...119 Look for the unusual ...120 Unusual time or place ...122 Dramatic irony ...125 Ending the feature ...126 Feature opportunities ...127 Feature example ...129

Chapter 8   Photographs 135

Something extra ...135 Size ...136 Picture quality ...136 Picture costs ...137 Group photos ...138 Vertical composition ...141 Something different ...142 Writing cutlines ...145 Policy taboos ...147

Chapter 9   Newspaper Organization 149

A general view ...149 Where do you come in? ...150 Editing copy ...152

Glossary 156

Index 160

Introduction

There is an aphorism I learned as a schoolboy: "Local government serves local needs." Also serving local needs are the social, civic and service organizations which abound in any community. These organizations collect blood, donate books to the town library, provide ambulance services, undertake civic improvements, monitor the local government and educational systems, and the list goes on and on.

To make the public aware of their activities, these organizations rely on the local newspaper to publicize their events and projects. The paper for which I work devotes a great deal of space in each edition to publicizing the activities of local organizations, from the PTA to the United Way.

No newspaper has enough reporters to assign to every activity of every organization; nor could newspapers afford to hire and maintain such a large staff. Likewise, most organizations would find the services of a professional public relations person or agency too costly. Still, newspapers need news and worthwhile community organizations need publicity if their programs are to be effective. The question is how to satisfy both needs.

One answer has been to appoint someone within each organization to write news releases for the local press. But assigning a club publicity chairman, by itself, is not enough, unless the person assigned is willing and able to conform to at least some of the rules of journalism.

In the newspaper business, as in any other business, time is money. Time cannot be wasted on copy which deviates from the paper's format, ignores newspaper policy and style, is ambiguous, incomplete, and which almost always is much, much longer than it needs to be (newspaper space is valuable).

Some stories are submitted in longhand and often are thrown away because no one on the news staff finds time to type them or because no one can decipher the author's hieroglyphics. There are many other journalistic infractions which either disqualify stories for publication or result in dull, ambiguous articles. Often, these infractions become a source of irritation to editors and make cooperation from the newspaper difficult to maintain.

This book was written to help beginning or part-time news writers not only get stories into their local newspapers, but to give those stories at least a touch of professionalism which will make them more effective by being clear, concise and easy to read. Also it may help bleary-eyed editors, such as myself, extend our sanity for a few years.

In addition to the local housewife who does publicity for the PTA, this book may be of help to those in full-time publicity jobs. Many eleemosynary organizations, for example, may be unable to afford professional PR representatives and assign publicity tasks instead to a person who may have good command of English but be unschooled in the requirements of journalism.

Those who serve regularly as club publicity chairmen and those who find full-time jobs as public relations writers will find this book useful as a ready reference. Organizations may want to keep several copies on hand to assign along with the "PR" title; colleges may consider using it as part of a writing course to give their students a taste of journalistic style. In addition, newspaper editors may recommend the book to their stringers, people who cover regular news beats in smaller towns on the fringe of the circulation area, who may have no formal journalism training.

One unusual feature of this book is its use of the hometown newspaper as a model, showing the reader what to look for there, rather than trying to memorize a list of inviolable rules. This approach is essential in dealing with the myriad styles and policies which abound among newspapers across the country.

I have tried to be selective. I have not attempted to cram four years of journalism training between these covers. This book may not succeed in getting your article about the Boy Scout picnic space on page one, but it should help you to write more professional news stories, which will increase their chances of being published and will help publicize the activities of your club.

1

Materials

THE TYPEWRITER

The traditional image of a newspaper office, I suppose, is a room full of clattering typewriters. While computer technology is changing that image somewhat (many large newspapers use computer terminals and keyboards) the typewriter remains one of the basic tools of journalism, and for good reason.

First, stories written in longhand are difficult to decipher—often for the author himself—and increase the probability of error and misunderstanding. Names are especially difficult to figure out. Errors are difficult enough to control in newspaper work without having handwritten stories to compound the problem.

Second, stories written in longhand must be typed, sooner or later. (Typesetters usually work against the clock and handwritten copy would slow down their production.) If no one on the busy news staff finds time for the task, your meeting will go unannounced or your project unpublicized.

If you are going to write news releases, then you should own or have access to a typewriter. Obviously, you may borrow one from a friend or a relative, or perhaps the organization for which you are writing will provide a typewriter for your use. Some libraries have typing rooms for public use. In fact, the newspaper in which you plan to run your story may have an idle machine which you may use.

Alternatively, you or your organization may want to rent a typewriter, which may be worth the expense if you are planning a heavy publicity campaign over a short period.

In most cases, however, it is advisable for you to own a machine. You probably will be the publicity chairman for at least one year. Besides, typewriters are useful in any family, especially ones in which there are students.

BUYING A TYPEWRITER

If you do decide to buy a typewriter, there are some things you should know to keep the purchase from becoming unnecessarily expensive.

Some machines, for example, have features which are useful in commercial operations. Options like cartridges instead of standard spool-fed ribbons and interchangeable type may be *nice* to have, but you probably will not *need* them for your purposes and the additional cost cannot be justified.

The price of a typewriter is well within the financial reach of most families. One discount catalogue I consulted listed a lightweight portable for around $40. But beware of "bargains."

You should, of course, be allowed to try the machine in the store. Look for a solid touch when you strike the keys and avoid cheap models which feel tinny, as they may prove unreliable and more expensive in the long run than a costlier machine of better quality.

Also, consider buying a re-conditioned machine from an office supply store. The machine upon which the manuscript for this book was prepared is a standard office typewriter which I bought used for $75.

By a "standard" machine, I mean a non-portable, desk typewriter of the kind a secretary in a business office might use. The weight of these machines keeps them from moving about as you type, but, more important, they are durable enough to give you many years of service.

Electric typewriters are more expensive than their non-electric counterparts. A good quality electric portable typewriter will cost in the neighborhood of $200. Electric machines are less fatiguing when a great deal of typing is involved—as in typing the manuscript for this book, for example.

On the other hand, the touch of an electric typewriter takes some getting used to, and you probably will not realize the advantages of an electric machine in typing only an occasional news release consisting of one or two pages.

Whatever kind of machine you choose, it is wise to stick to established brands; otherwise, you may have trouble finding replacement ribbons and parts.

There are some other features to look for in judging the quality of a machine. The case should be of a gauge thick enough to ensure protection of the mechanisms within it. The roller should turn with solid clicks and not slip or bind. The keys should strike the paper firmly and squarely, producing straight lines of type instead of lines in which the letters register at various heights.

Pica or elite type is recommended over all other styles. Script type, which resembles handwriting, for example, may be acceptable for writing letters to friends, but it is too hard on the eyes to be appreciated by newspaper editors.

TYPEWRITER MAINTENANCE

Once you acquire a typewriter, it is important to keep it in good repair through proper maintenance. It does not take a mechanical genius to keep keys free from dust and ink, and ribbons are not so expensive that they cannot be changed when the ink fades.

Not only will simple maintenance help to extend the life of your machine, but you will win the tacit approval of your local copy editor by not making him guess whether he is looking at an "e" or an "o" or trying to read copy prepared by a worn-out ribbon which renders the material nearly invisible.

Your local stationery store will be able to supply you with the proper ribbon and cleaning supplies for your typewriter. Special brushes, solvents and cleaning gums and papers are available.

If you do not have a typewriter brush, an old toothbrush will work just as well. You can even use household rubbing alcohol as a solvent. Dip your brush in a small amount of alcohol, shake off the excess, and brush over the keys, reaching all the nooks and crannies. Then blot the keys with bathroom or facial tissue.

RIBBONS AND PAPERS

Traditionally, newspapers have been published in black and white. While colored inks and color pictures are becoming popular, the use of colors in preparing news story manuscripts still is verboten.

Use a solid black ribbon. You will have no need for red or any other color.

Likewise, use only white paper. The objection, as

before, is that colors are too hard on the eyes. In addition, colored ribbons and papers are sure signs of an amateur.

Furthermore, the paper you use should be standard 8½ × 11-inch typing bond and should be unlined. The paper need not be expensive; in fact, newspapers cut the end rolls of their newsprint—a cheap grade of paper—for use in the newsroom.

I also caution against the use of some brands of erasable paper which are dirty to work with. They are so slippery that the ink smears at the slightest touch. These brands often are difficult to paste together, which is a problem for newspapers which send their copy to the composing room by gluing all the pages of a story into one strip, rather than in "takes."

TYPOGRAPHICAL ERRORS

Actually, there are ways of correcting typographical errors in news stories which make erasable paper unnecessary.

The simplest way to correct an error is to "xxx" through it. Re-type the correct word or letter above or immediately after the error. The need to correct errors is one reason why, in the next chapter, you will be told to double space your stories.

You also may use correction tape or correction fluid or simply erase.

You may want to use proofreaders' marks, which editors use to correct errors. Some dictionaries— *Webster's New Collegiate* is one—list these marks in the appendix. The slash, which is used to delete words or letters, and the caret, which is used for insertions, are especially useful.

To delete: lett⁄er

To insert: leťer or leťer

OTHER MATERIALS

In addition to the materials we have discussed so far, you probably will need some method of taking notes and you should keep copies of the stories you have written.

The availability of inexpensive cassette tape recorders has made them popular tools for some reporters. Still, there are limitations to their use. Some subjects object to being taped or become self-conscious, and if you are reciting your notes into the recorder during a meeting, the chairman may decide that you are distracting the group's attention and request that you stop.

Most reporters still rely on taking notes by hand. Some reporters use a stenographer's pad, some prefer a spiral or loose-leaf notebook, and others simply use a few sheets of typing paper. Notebooks can be whatever size and shape seems handiest for you.

As far as writing instruments are concerned, I find the mechanical pencil to be most dependable. You may prefer an ordinary graphite pencil (make sure you have at least one spare), a felt-tip pen, or a ballpoint.

MAKING COPIES

It is a good idea to make copies of the stories you write.

A file of stories you have submitted has many uses. It documents to the organization the effort and volume of your work. It also is a good reference when writing future stories on the same subject. Furthermore, should the newspaper lose your copy, you will have no difficulty in providing a duplicate quickly. Finally, should the newspaper office telephone to clear up a point, your copy will be handy to determine the exact wording the reporter or editor has before him.

Another reason for making a copy is to compare

your original story with the way it finally appears in print. If there are changes, there is a good chance the reason for the change will be covered in this book. But, do not be alarmed if your story does not appear exactly as you wrote it. Even stories written by staff reporters are changed to some degree. Most changes probably will involve style, which will be covered in Chapter 3.

By double checking your stories, you will begin to develop the style and tone your newspaper prefers. Copies also will provide you with a record of your releases so you can keep your stories fresh when you are writing a series of articles on the same subject.

Remember, however, never to submit a carbon or a photocopy to a newspaper; submit only the original. There will be further discussion on this point in Chapter 4.

BRIEF REVIEW

The purpose of this chapter is to acquaint you with the use and maintenance of the typewriter and introduce you to some other materials you will use to write your news stories.

Before going on to the next chapter, then, let us review some salient points:

—Always use a typewriter to write news releases.

—Pica and elite type faces are recommended over all others.

—Keep the typewriter covered and free from dust and ink.

—Use only a solid black ribbon.

—Keep the ribbon fresh.

—Use white, unlined typing paper, 8½ × 11 inches, and avoid messy erasable brands.

2

Format

WHAT GOES WHERE

If you have written a business letter or even a letter to a friend, then you have followed some general format in which the date, the greeting, the complimentary close and the inside address, if there is one, all have a specific place on the page.

News stories, too, should be prepared according to a format, even if your local paper does not require it. Doing so will insure that you have provided the newspaper with all the information about release dates, distribution and other data that it needs to make editorial judgments about the piece.

Concomitantly, the use of a basic news format will give your stories a more professional appearance. Besides, if this is your first try at writing news stories, you may find that the structure gives you some confidence when you face that blank sheet of paper.

The format I suggest in this chapter is not the *only* way to set up a news story. Still, it is one which should be accepted by any newspaper. Examples of the format are provided at the end of this chapter and the end of Chapter 7.

What information does the editor need? First of all, he needs to know where the news release originates, the name of your organization. He needs to know the date it was prepared, to determine its timeliness. Another vital bit of information is a contact he can call if there are questions about the release. Whether you are submitting a story to the *New York Times* or the *Weekly Bugle,* your press release must contain this information. To emphasize again, I will present the format my paper requires. Other newspapers may not require as much information. It is up to you to find out the requirements of the papers to which you send material.

For the sake of illustration, let us suppose that you are publicity chairman for the Franklin Street Elementary School PTA and that the president has asked you to announce that the PTA will buy encyclopedias for the school library.

You have made sure that your typewriter keys are clean and that the ribbon is not worn. Your paper is in place and you are ready to begin.

SLUGGING A STORY

The first piece of information which you will put on the page is called a "slug." The slug helps the editor to identify your story.

For the story in the situation I suggested above, an appropriate slug would be: encyclopedias.

The slug will be typed in the upper left-hand corner of the page, about eight to 10 spaces from the top.

The slug must be specific enough to avoid confusion with similar pieces. "Encyclopedias" probably is uncommon enough to stand alone, but many organizations hold rummage sales, for example, and in cases where confusion may occur, include part of your organization's name in the slug: Franklin rummage sale.

DISTRIBUTION LINE

One of the first things your local editor will want to know is who else is receiving a copy of your release. You tell him in a distribution line, which will be typed three or four spaces directly under the slug.

You do not have to tell your local editor that you have sent a copy of your story to your Aunt Tillie, but the newspaper business is highly competitive and he will certainly want to know if any other papers or the local TV and radio stations will receive copies.

Any newspaperman worth his salt wants to "scoop" the competition, radio and television included. Many papers insist that releases be submitted to them and to them alone.

If the papers in your area prohibit multiple submissions, you will have to choose among them. You might use one paper on one occasion and another paper on the next.

You may be tempted to lie to the paper about the distribution of a story for fear your article will be rejected, but honesty is, as usual, the best policy. The newspaper for which I work has a "blacklist" of clubs which have lied about distribution. Stories from these clubs are automatically discarded and it may take months before they can convince the paper that they have repented.

Be prepared, then, to submit a story only to one paper in a given circulation area. Getting back to the subject of this section, your distribution line would read: "exclusive to the *Daily Bugle*" or whatever the name of your local paper happens to be.

Remember to be truthful. If you send the same story

to two papers in the same circulation area, list both names in the distribution line. For example: "copies to the *Daily Bugle* and *The Evening News.*"

It is always best to submit a story exclusively to one paper, however, because if you send the story to several papers, each may decide that the competition will break it first and all will discard it.

Most papers will not object to a story being sent to papers in other circulation areas. If that is the case, you may write in your distribution line: "exclusive in your area."

Also tell the editor if the story you have sent to him has been sent to the local radio and/or television stations. Some papers may not object to that. If such is the case, your distribution line might read: "copies to *The Daily Bugle* and WXYZ-TV."

RELEASE DATE

Three or four spaces directly beneath the distribution line, type the most important piece of information in the format: the release date.

The release date is important because it tells the editor when your story will be most timely.

In most cases, the release date will be specific, like: "January 15," or "October 5." In the next chapter, "Style," we will discuss how some papers prefer to use words like "tomorrow" or "yesterday," in news stories rather than a specific date. Regardless, terms such as those should never appear in the release date. Let us examine the function of the release date more closely to find out why.

Let us say that you have prepared a news release which you hope to have published in the January 15 edition of the paper. If you wait until January 15 to file (submit) the story, you may find that the story is not used until a day or two later.

The reason is that many stories compete for space in each edition of the paper and the editor must decide how to "play" (display) them, where they will run, and when they will be used. Stories with the most news value, of course, will be used before other, more routine articles, which may be held back as long as the time element does not make them stale. It is especially important for editors whose newspapers use the "yesterday," "today" and "tomorrow" style to have some chronological reference point which gives those terms meaning.

If you specify a release date of January 15, for example, "tomorrow" will mean January 16; "today" will mean January 15; and "yesterday" will mean January 14. If the editor cannot schedule your story on the date you specify, he knows he must adjust those terms to compensate for the change.

It is always a good idea to get your stories to the paper a day or two before the release date you are shooting for. It is possible, then, barring any objection, to find your story used earlier than the specified release date.

If you specify a release date of January 15 and file your story on January 12, the editor may discover that he has a news "hole" to fill on January 13 or January 14 and he may use your story to plug it. Again, an adjustment may be necessary in the time reference to conform to style and accurately report the date of the event.

How far in advance you should file a story will vary from paper to paper. Inquire what "lead time," as it is called, is required by the paper you hope to use.

In most cases, then, your release date will read something like this: "for release on January 15," substituting, of course, the appropriate date.

In some stories, the time element may be unimportant. A feature story, for example, may be written in such a way that it may run at any time. In another case, a newspaper which publishes only once a week, on Sunday, perhaps, may prefer not to specify the date of events which occurred earlier in the week unless the date is germane to the story.

In stories where the time element is suspended, it is permissible to use for your release date: "for immediate release." This tells the editor that he may use the story at once or as soon as he is able to schedule it.

In "immediate release" stories you must use specific dates in the text (Jan. 4, Mar. 16, Oct. 2, for example) to avoid confusion.

If there is no rush to have a story in print, you may use something like the following as your release date: "release at your discretion."

You are telling the editor that there is no hurry to have the story published and the advantage is that the piece is likely to get better play if it is used on a day when news is light, rather than be squeezed in on some specific date when the news may be heavy. If you have written a good story, you can be sure that the editor will want to use it as soon as possible. If holding a story for several days will mean most prominent display, the wait is worth it.

There is one final situation regarding the release date which may have occurred to you as you discovered that stories might be used early. If a story must not be published before a certain date, after which it may be used at any time, you can inform the editor in a release date like the following: "for release after January 15" or "not for release before January 15." This type of instruction is called an embargo.

PERSONAL INFORMATION

In case the editor needs to contact you about a story, provide your name, address and telephone number. That information may be single spaced three or four lines below the release date.

Once you have included your personal information,

skip another four or five spaces and you are ready to
begin your story.

HEADLINES

Do not, as many publicity chairmen do, suggest a
headline for your story. You are wasting your time and I
know editors who view the practice as an annoying pre-
sumption on the part of the writer.

One of the duties of a copy editor is to write headlines, and chapters in textbooks have been devoted to the
proper construction of headlines. The task is not as
simple as it may seem. For one thing, the headline you
suggest may contain too many or too few characters to fit
the type of head designated by the chief copy editor.

You need not and should not write your own headlines. The slug at the top of the page is sufficient.

SPACE FOR THE EDITOR

If you follow the format I have outlined, your story
will begin about one-third down the page. This leaves
room in the upper right-hand corner for the editor to give
headline and typographical instructions to the copy
editors and composing room personnel.

In addition, you must leave space for the editors to
make changes and corrections in your story.

Before beginning your story, make sure that your
space selector is set at least for double spacing. Triple
spacing is even better. This will allow both you and the
editor enough room between lines to make corrections.
Single-spaced copy is accepted with weeping, wailing and
gnashing of teeth, if it is accepted at all.

You also must leave editing room in the left and
right margins. Set your paper guide so that the left edge
of the paper is under zero on the carriage bar. Move your

carriage to "15" and set the left margin; then, to "65" or "70" and set the right-hand margin.

Once you set the right-hand margin, the carriage will be extended to the left. With the carriage in that position, locate the "tab clear" button on your machine and holding it down return the carriage to the right until it stops. Indent five to seven spaces and press and release the button marked "tab set." This automatically sets the paragraph indentation. Each time you are ready to begin a new paragraph, you will need only to depress the button marked "tab" or "tabular."

Once you begin your story, continue to within one inch or one and one-half inches from the bottom of the page. A light pencil mark will keep you from going too far. Judge your work so that you do not end a page in the middle of a sentence or a paragraph. Do not begin a paragraph that cannot be completed on the same page.

If you will have another page, skip two more spaces below the last line, center the carriage and type "--more--." This tells the copy editor that there is more than one page to your story.

On the second page, if one is necessary, leave about five spaces at the top and type in the upper left-hand corner "first add" and the slug. In the illustration I gave earlier, for example, you would write: "first add--encyclopedias." Skip another four or five spaces and continue with your story. (Some papers use "add 1" instead of "first add.")

If your story will have three pages, type "--more--" in the bottom margin of page two. In the upper left-hand corner of page three you would write "second add--encyclopedias." The procedure repeats for each succeeding page.

If your story ends on page three, type "second and final add--encyclopedias" in the upper left-hand corner. (See example at end of Chapter 7.)

When you have typed the final line of your story,

skip two lines, center the carriage and write "30" (the traditional newspaper ending) or "end" or use the symbol "##" to indicate the conclusion of the article.

Using sequential numerical "adds" eliminates any need to fasten the pages of an article together. If you insist on fastening the pages, however, *never* use staples or dog-ear corners. Use paper clips.

TWO MORE TABOOS

There are two additional "don'ts" to keep in mind before moving on to Chapter 3.

First, never type your stories entirely in capital letters. Second, never type on both sides of the paper.

Typing a story entirely in capital letters supposedly makes copy prepared for radio or television easier to read over the air. (Actually, it doesn't). In newspaper writing, this favorite practice of non-professionals means extra work for the editors, who must put two or three short lines under every letter which is to be capitalized before the copy is sent to the composing room. (One supposes the novice types in capitals so he won't have to make decisions on what letters to capitalize.)

The second taboo is less common but just as objectionable. Material typed on the reverse side of a page must be retyped or photocopied before the story can be set in type. Some newspapers may not take the trouble to recopy the reverse-side material, using only the information on the first side or discarding the piece altogether.

Following the suggestions contained in this chapter helps to eliminate the kind of busy work which drives editors up the wall. Busy work is not only annoying but also leaves the editor with less time to apply the finer points of journalism for which he has been trained.

Before moving on, consider again the highlights of this chapter:

—Use the recommended format to provide all the

information an editor will need to process your
story and to allow him space for instructions to the
printers.

—Never write your own headline.

—Double space or triple space your story.

—Leave adequate margins at the bottom of each
page as well as to the right and left.

—Use sequentially numbered "adds" with the slug
on all additional pages.

—Use "more" to indicate additional pages and "30,"
"end," or "##" to indicate the conclusion of an
article.

—Use paper clips to fasten pages; never use staples.

—Never type a story entirely in capitals.

—Never type on both sides of the paper.

SAMPLE FORMAT

—10 spaces from top—

Encyclopedias   **(slug)**

—three to four spaces—

Exclusive to The Daily News   (distribution line)

—three to four spaces—

For release Jan. 15   (release date)

—three to four spaces—

Your Name   (personal information)
Your Street
Your Town
Your telephone number

—four to five spaces—

**Begin your story. Double space and allow adequate
margins to the left and right. If your story will consist of
only one page, continue to within about one inch from
the bottom of the page and write "--30--" or "end" or
use the symbol "##" at the bottom center of the page.
If you will need more than one page, write "--more--"
where I have written "--30--" below. The example at the
end of Chapter 7 shows you how to slug adds.**

—two spaces—
—30—

3

News Style

WHAT IS NEWS STYLE?

With this discussion of news style, we begin to consider the more substantive aspects of journalism. The information presented here and in the next two chapters will lay the groundwork for actual construction of the news story, which we will take up in Chapter 6.

To begin with, style in journalism does not have the same meaning as it does in literature. Style in literature is the way the writer constructs his sentences and chooses his words—how he uses the language—which gives his narrative a characteristic flow and rhythm.

Ernest Hemingway, for example, wrote in a terse style which was far different from the complex, rambling style of Henry James.

Whether you realize it or not, you already have acquired a writing style in the literary sense. This style has been shaped by the kinds of books you read, the essays you studied in English class, and even your dinner table conversation. Chances are that you speak and write very much like your friends and relatives.

In the literary sense, style in journalism is more like Hemingway than James. In fact, after Hemingway graduated from high school he worked as a reporter on the *Kansas City Star.*

The goal in news writing is for short, simple sentences (like Hemingway's) which present to the reader a series of facts in as direct a manner as possible. Your news style in the literary sense will evolve, I hope, as you apply the information which will be presented in the chapters to follow.

But style has another meaning in journalism. Style in journalism consists of a body of rules which dictate how certain recurring words, phrases and grammatical constructions are to be written in order to achieve uniformity within any given publication.

Usually, these rules are set down in a *stylebook,* which instructs the reporter on how to prepare copy, the newspaper's preferences on use of punctuation, capitalization and abbreviations.

Newspapers are said to conform generally to the "up" or "down" style of capitalization. In the "up" style, all parts of a proper noun are capitalized: Grant High School, Finance Committee of the Kenosha City Council, etc. In the "down" style, only the proper noun itself is capitalized: Grant high school, finance committee of the Kenosha city council, etc. Some papers have a modification of the two styles and these are spelled out in the stylebook.

Some papers insist on spelling out the word "street," as in "Main Street," and some prefer abbreviations— "Main St."

The stylebook also may dictate the use or omission of polite forms of address like "Mr." and "Mrs." Reporters are told how to write dates and times of events, or whether to write out a number or use a figure.

What is important to remember is that style is not a matter of correct and incorrect in strict grammatical terms. It is more a matter of preference. Moreover, just as the literary styles of Hemingway and James differed considerably, so will newspaper styles vary among newspapers across the country.

If you expect to write news stories on a regular basis, I would advise you to contact your local paper to see if you can obtain a copy of its stylebook. Stylebooks need be no more elaborate than mimeographed sheets stapled together and I truly believe that making stylebooks available to organization publicity chairmen would benefit small papers which rely on non-professional or non-staff writers for much of their news. The time required to edit stories for style would be reduced considerably.

If your local paper uses the United Press International news service, the Associated Press, or some other news service, chances are that its style will conform to that of the service it uses. Still, you may find local exceptions to wire service style. For example, the paper for which I work uses United Press International but deviates from UPI style by capitalizing the names of the seasons, a style established by a former publisher.

Many of the examples I use in this chapter are based upon the UPI style and should represent a fair consensus of most newspapers' preferences, but keep in mind that there may be local exceptions.

If you cannot obtain a copy of your local paper's stylebook, you still have a reference as close as your front porch. Your newspaper itself may be used as a stylebook.

Use this chapter as a guide to help you identify examples of style in your local paper and begin to compile a stylebook of your own. It may be as simple or as elaborate as you choose. You may, quite simply, circle examples of style in an old copy of your paper and fold it away somewhere for future reference, or you might paste examples under specific categories in a loose-leaf notebook. In this chapter, I will cover five categories of style: date-time groups; polite forms of address; professional, official and military titles; abbreviations; and numbers.

DATES AND TIMES

Style is largely a matter of preference but this first illustration shows that there are often practical reasons for choosing one style over another.

In the case of dates and times, style is used to avoid confusion in the event of a typographical error. In considering the following example, it may occur to you that you have taken a great deal for granted as far as what is required to write for newspapers is concerned.

There are several different ways of saying that a certain event will occur on a certain day at a certain time. We might write that an event will occur "on Tuesday night at 8" or "at 8 on Tuesday night." Neither of these styles is more correct than the other. Both styles, however, are preferable to a style which uses "A.M." and "P.M." to set the time of day.

The objection to "A.M." and "P.M." is a practical one. The use of those designations may lead to confusion in the event of a typographical error.

There is no such thing as a "perfect copy" of a newspaper. Deadlines make typographical perfection impractical, if not impossible.

If you write that an event will take place "on Tuesday at 8 P.M." and the phrase is erroneously set in type as "on Tuesday at 8 X.M.," the reader cannot be certain if the event will occur in the morning or at night.

On the other hand, if you write the date and time in

the style "on Tuesday *night* at 8" and a typographical error renders "on Tuesday xight at 8," the meaning still is obvious.

It is possible, too, that some newspapers still may be using "o'clock" in date-time groups, but, because "o'clock" is superfluous, most papers avoid it.

Now inspect your local paper *thoroughly* to see how dates and times are written. I stress *thoroughly* because some papers with small staffs may not be able to spend a great deal of time editing copy for style. In addition, there may be instances where the rules of style will be violated inadvertently, so you must examine the entire paper carefully to establish the newspaper's preference in a majority of cases.

Having dealt with the style for writing the time of day, we now examine variations used in designating the day of the week. In examining your local paper for style, you may find that days are written as a specific date (Jan. 15); or, perhaps, the newspaper uses the day (Tuesday, Friday, etc.). You may even find "yesterday," "today," and "tomorrow" being used.

What designation you will use for the day of the week will depend upon your release date, which was discussed in Chapter 2.

When an event will occur within one day on either side of the release date or on the release date itself, it is common to find the "yesterday, today and tomorrow" style being used.

If your release date is January 15 and you are writing about an event which will be held on that day, you might write something like: "The PTA will meet *tonight* at 8." If the event will take place on the following day, January 16, you would write: "The PTA will meet *tomorrow night* at 8."

Usually, this style is modified slightly for events which occurred on the day before the release date. In most cases, the hour at which a past event occurred is immaterial and many papers omit the reference. You would write: "The PTA met last night," omitting the hour.

Other uses of the "yesterday, today and tomorrow" style are illustrated in the following example.

Example 1
PTA President John Doe said *yesterday* that . . . .
At a meeting *last night*, the Franklin Street Elementary PTA voted to. . . .
The Franklin Street Elementary PTA will decide *tomorrow* whether or not to. . . .

In using designations such as these, keep in mind that morning usually means the period from immediately after midnight up to but not including noon. Afternoon is usually the period from immediately after noon to 5 P.M. (the latter may vary). Evening may mean from 5 to 6:30, with night usually beginning at 7.

Furthermore, "midnight" and "noon" stand alone, without the figure "12." The figure is superfluous. Also eliminate the double zero after the colon when writing times on the hour. For example, write "5" instead of "5:00." Of course, you will still write "5:30," "2:45," "8:15," and so on, but the double zero adds nothing.

Keep in mind, however, that your newspaper may prefer to use the specific date in all cases, rather than the "yesterday-today-tomorrow" style. Even when the latter style is used, it must be suspended, or at least modified, for events which will occur more than one week from the date of publication.

If your release date is January 15, a Monday, for example, and you are writing about an event which will occur on January 24, a Wednesday, you have to write that the event will occur on "Wednesday, January 24." You may drop the day if you like, but not the date. If you use "Wednesday" without the date, you are referring to Wednesday, January 17.

Check your local paper to see if it prefers both day and date or just the date in situations of this type.

Style also will dictate whether or not to abbreviate the name of the month. The UPI stylebook which my paper uses abbreviates the names of all months except March, April, May, June and July. Names of months usually are written out if the month and year are used without a date and when a month stands alone.

Example 2
It began in October, 1921.
Meetings will resume in September.

It also is unnecessary to use the current year as part of the date.

Finally, in following style you will use either "night" or "P.M." but never both in the same phrase. The same is true for "morning" and "A.M." If you write "on Friday morning at 8 A.M." you are actually saying "on Friday morning at 8 in the morning." The construction is redundant. Also avoid superfluous constructions like "the *month* of June." Everyone knows that June is a month.

POLITE ADDRESS

One of the easiest rules of style to recognize is the use or omission of Mr., Mrs., Miss and Ms. The trend has been to eliminate Mr. and Ms. because they tell the reader nothing about the person to whom they refer. The style question is simple: either these titles are used or they are not.

Mrs. and Miss, however, still are commonly used because they tell the reader what a woman's marital status is.

The paper for which I work identifies a male initially as "John Doe," for example, and refers to him as "Doe" from then on. We also use Miss and Mrs., referring to a woman initially as "Miss Jane Doe" or "Mrs. John Doe" and subsequently as "Miss Doe" or "Mrs. Doe."

The recent women's liberation movement use of Ms. has created a minor style problem.

Lately, we have been receiving stories which refer to females as "Ms. Jane Doe." Since we do not use "Mr.," we must follow style and eliminate "Ms." "Ms. Jane Doe" becomes "Jane Doe," subsequently referred to as "Doe," just as we identify a male.

I must admit that my male chauvinism, I suppose, made me quite uncomfortable about referring to a woman as "Doe" but I have grown used to the style now.

My paper still uses Mrs. and Miss when they are offered but I quite agree that a woman's marital status is no more relevant to a news story than a man's. My inclination is to eliminate these polite forms altogether. At any rate, consistency in style is what is important. If Mr. is not used, Ms. should not be used either.

Mr. and Mrs. still are used when referring to a husband and wife together: "Mr. and Mrs. John Doe" and "Mr. and Mrs. Doe."

There are two final points I want to make concerning names.

First, no matter how well you know a person, *never* refer to him by his or her first name alone. If you refer to a person initially as "John Doe," thereafter, call him "Doe" and not "John," even if he is your brother. There are instances in feature stories and stories concerning young children where first names are used instead of family names.

Second, never familiarly shorten a person's name. If his name is "Thomas," for example, refer to him as "Thomas Doe" and not as "Tom Doe."

In situations where a person is formally known by a shortened form of his name, however, an exception is made. Such would be the case with singer Tom Jones, for example, comedian Jackie Gleason, or President Jimmy Carter.

PROFESSIONAL TITLES

Unlike the polite forms of address, professional, official and military titles are relevant pieces of information. Titles tell the reader something about their holders.

Broadly speaking, titles designate authority, and designating authority is important in news writing, as will be discussed in Chapter 5 and Chapter 6.

In compiling your stylebook, carefully note if your local paper abbreviates titles in all cases, or if it abbreviates in some cases and spells the title out in others. Also note where the title is placed. Some papers always place the title in front of the name, others prefer to use the title after the name, and still others use the title before the name in some cases and after the name in others. In addition, some papers drop the title after the initial reference and others carry the title throughout.

You may find, for example, that one paper refers to a physician as "Dr. Jane Doe," and subsequently as "Dr. Doe." Other papers may make subsequent reference to her as just "Doe."

If you find that the title is neither consistently retained nor consistently omitted in subsequent references, the choice is up to you. You can refer to the person as "Dr. Doe" in some places and as "Doe" in others.

You may find that the paper with which you are dealing prefers a style which distinguishes between physicians and other persons who appropriately could be called "doctor."

In such cases, style may dictate that the title be placed after the name instead of before it. For example, a physician may be referred to as "John Doe, M.D.," rather than "Dr. John Doe." Likewise, a dentist might be referred to as "John Doe, D.D.S.," and a person who holds a doctor of philosophy degree would be called "John Doe, Ph.D.," instead of "Dr. John Doe." Style also will dictate whether or not to use periods in abbreviations; for example, "M.D." or "MD."

Variations like these deserve noting in your stylebook.

Usually, "Dr." always is abbreviated. Exceptions would be rare. Still, some styles may require that certain titles be spelled out when they are used with the surname alone in subsequent references.

To illustrate, a legislator may be introduced as "Sen. John Doe," and referred to subsequently as "Senator Doe," with his title spelled out, rather than "Sen. Doe." Either style may prevail in your area, so this is another item for your stylebook.

Whatever the style, when using titles be careful to avoid redundancies. You may write "Dr. John Doe" or "John Doe, M.D.," but never "Dr. John Doe, M.D."

However, there may be cases where two titles are appropriate; if so, both may be used. If a clergyman, for example, also holds a doctor of divinity degree, he may be referred to as "The Rev. John Doe, D.D." In this case, "Rev." and "D.D." do not mean the same thing.

In writing about clergymen, there is another point of style to bear in mind. The UPI stylebook dictates that "Rev." is not to be used without "the" preceding it. Some papers follow this rule, others do not. Note the preference of your local paper in your stylebook.

The use of clerical titles also varies among religions. Thus, a Protestant clergyman is referred to as "the Rev. John Doe" and "the Reverend Doe" or "the Rev. Doe," while a Catholic priest is called "the Rev. John Doe" and "Father Doe."

In addition to these examples, the UPI stylebook cites other usages for various religions. The following are based on the stylebook and illustrate the initial reference, followed by the subsequent reference.

Example 3
Roman Catholic:
    The Rt. Rev. Msgr. John Doe; Father Doe.
    The Most Rev. John Doe, bishop of the Scranton Diocese; Bishop Doe.
    John Cardinal Doe; Cardinal Doe.
    A nun whose name is Doe is called by her church name—Sister Mary Joseph, for example—and is never referred to as Sister Doe.
Espiscopal:
    A deacon or priest is referred to as the Rev. John Doe; the Rev. Mr. Doe.
    A dean is the Very Rev. John Doe; the Rev. Mr. Doe or Dean Doe.
    A bishop is the Rt. Rev. John Doe; the Rev. Mr. Doe or Bishop Doe.
    Some priests use the term "Father," which is permissible but not generally used.
Jewish:
    Rabbi John Doe; Rabbi Doe or Dr. Doe, where degree is held.
    Cantor John Doe; Cantor Doe.
    Do not identify a rabbi as a "Reverend Doctor."
Christian Science:
    Practitioner, Lecturer, Reader. Do not use "Rev." in any form.
    Reader John Doe of the First Church.
Lutheran:
    Pastor John Doe; Pastor Doe or Mr. Doe.
Latter-day Saints (Mormon):
    President John Doe; President Doe.
    Elder John Doe; Elder Doe.
    Presiding Bishop John Doe; Bishop Doe.

OFFICIAL TITLES

Every organization is run by a group of officers. Furthermore, organizations of the type to which you belong frequently have public officials who appear as guest speakers.

With regard to the placement of the title before or after the name and the retention of the title in subsequent references, official titles generally follow the same rules which apply to professional titles. You may refer to "President John Doe," for example, or "John Doe, president of the PTA." You may call him "President Doe" and refer to him thereafter as "Doe."

The same holds true for the vice president (style may require vice-president with a hyphen), the secretary and the treasurer (or in some cases secretary-treasurer).

Abbreviations, however, are another matter. Usually, these official titles are not abbreviated. It is rare to find "Pres. John Doe," for example.

In dealing with organization officers, there is one construction to be avoided: Never say, "President John Doe presided." "President" means "presiding officer," which makes this construction superfluous. Nevertheless, it is a favorite among non-professional publicity writers.

A similar objection is raised to the explanation that: "Vice President John Smith presided in the absence of President John Doe." It is the duty of the vice president to preside in the absence of the president and so this construction, too, is superfluous. Note these two objections in your stylebook.

MILITARY TITLES

The UPI stylebook lists preferred abbreviations for military ranks but these abbreviations will vary drastically from place to place and it would be a waste of time to list them here. Study your local paper and compile a list of these abbreviations for your stylebook.

One thing to remember about military titles, or any

other titles, for that matter, is that a title or position is not capitalized when it stands apart from a person's name. For example, you would write "Capt. John Doe" but "John Doe, a captain," or "He was a captain in the Army." There is a special section on capitalization in Chapter 5.

In addition, the names of United States military services usually are capitalized: Army, Navy, Marines, Air Force, Coast Guard and National Guard, for example.

ABBREVIATIONS

Abbreviations comprise another major category of style. You already have seen how abbreviations are used in titles and you should be alert to whether or not periods are used or omitted.

A frequent decision you will have to make on abbreviations is whether or not to abbreviate thoroughfare designations.

Some newspapers write "Main Street," for example, and others prefer "Main St." "Down" style is "Main street," with a lower case "s" and it is conceivable that there might even be a "Main st." style.

The UPI stylebook recommends the abbreviation of street (St.), avenue (Ave.), boulevard (Blvd.), and terrace (Ter.) in addresses, but not point, port, circle, plaza, place, drive, oval, road, or lane. Using this style, you would write "Main St." but "Columbus Circle."

In addition to recording in your stylebook the preference for abbreviating or not abbreviating thoroughfare designations, you have to consider, too, if your paper abbreviates directional references. Does style require "East Main St.," "East Main Street," or E. Main St.," for example?

Newspapers commonly use abbreviations for the names of organizations, firms, agencies and other groups. It is good practice to write out the name of an organization the first time it is mentioned in a story; thereafter, it is permissible to use the official abbreviation. You might mention the Federal Bureau of Investigation, for example, and refer to that agency subsequently as the FBI.

Some organizations are widely known by their initials: CIA, GOP, PTA, AFL-CIO. In fact, AFL-CIO is preferred over American Federation of Labor and Congress of Industrial Organizations. Local style may allow still other abbreviations that are well known in your particular area. The Salt River Project, for example, is well known in Phoenix as SRP. Try to keep the news columns from turning into alphabet soup.

It used to be that the abbreviation for an obscure organization was listed in parentheses after the organization's name: The Society for the Protection and Preservation of Warthogs (SPPW). The practice now is discouraged. The United Press International stylebook says if the abbreviation of an organization's name is not by itself sufficient to identify the organization, then the abbreviation should not be used at all.

I already have pointed out that official titles like president and vice president are seldom abbreviated. The UPI stylebook contains a list of other words which should not be abbreviated unless local style dictates otherwise: port, association, point, detective, department, deputy, commandant, commodore, field marshal, general manager, secretary-general, and, above all, Christmas. Nor should days of the week be abbreviated, except in tabular matter.

HOW TO WRITE NUMBERS

Writing numbers often presents a problem for non-professionals: when to write out numbers and when to use figures.

The most basic rule is to write out all numbers from one to nine and to use numerals for all numbers from 10 on. There are some exceptions and special cases, however, which we will consider.

Usually, the over-and-under-10 rule is suspended when writing dates and times, when a number is the first word in a sentence, and depending upon local style, when writing ages.

I am confident, for example, that you have never seen "Jan. First" in a newspaper. Nor are you likely to see a sentence which begins: "60 people . . ." In such cases, style will be "Jan. 1" and "Sixty people," contrary to the over-and-under-10 rule.

It also is common to find "Thursday night at 8" instead of "Thursday night at eight" and some papers prefer to use "a boy, 6," rather than "a boy, six." Note such variations in your stylebook.

LARGE NUMBERS

The over-and-under-10 rule for numbers applies up to and including 999,999. For numbers beyond 999,999, it is common to use a kind of shorthand which makes numbers easier to grasp.

Using an extreme case, which is easier to grasp: "15 trillion" or "15,000,000,000,000"?

The rule for numbers over and under 10 applies to this shorthand form: "one" trillion and not "1" trillion. Always remember, though, to check local style.

Large numbers are often rounded off and expressed as a decimal, unless there is some reason to use the exact figure. More often than not, you will find a number like 222,789,651 written as 2.2 million. ("2.2" is less than 10, but because it consists of two digits, it is not written out. Similarly, the dollar sign is considered a digit, suspending the over-and-under-10 rule in monetary amounts, as you will see in a moment.)

MONETARY FIGURES

Upon occasion, you will have to write amounts of money. Usually, the over-and-under-10 rule does not apply, the preference being to use numbers preceded by a dollar sign: $1, $10, $500,000, $2 million, $2.5 million.

The over-and-under-10 rule, however, usually is applied to amounts of money under $1: two cents, nine cents, 10 cents, 78 cents.

PERCENTAGES

Percentages represent another class of numbers which presents a problem of style. The decision usually is over whether to write out the percentage or use a figure and the percent sign (%).

Check local style to see if "1%" or "one percent" is preferred.

The over-and-under-10 rule may be suspended for percentages as it is for dollar amounts. The reason is that the "%" and "$" take the place of a number. Thus, you will find: "4%" "2.5%" and "62%."

The UPI-AP stylebook, however, says that "an isolated one-time reference" involving a number under 10 is to be spelled out; for example: "According to a recent poll, only four percent of the PTA supports . . . ." If, however, you will be including many percentage citations in your story, use the figure and percent sign style.

Furthermore, it is possible that you will find "percent" written out with a number, but seldom the converse; for example, "12 percent" but never "one %."

In addition, some newspapers will not use the figure and percent sign style within a direct quotation. The reasoning usually is that people do not speak in numbers and symbols. A few papers use the same reasoning for numbers in direct quotations, so check local style and note the preference in your stylebook.

FRACTIONS

Most good typewriters carry a fraction key for ½ and ¼. Note the local style requirement for these and other fractions when they appear.

Some newspapers, for example, use a slash to indicate a fraction like 3/4. If the fraction is part of a mixed number, the fraction may be linked to the whole number with a hyphen: 10-3/4.

When fractions are written alone, they usually are spelled out: *three-fourths* of the class and *one-half* of an apple, for example.

Some newspapers may prefer "one and one-half" to "1½." However, I cannot overemphasize that style is not a question of what is correct or incorrect. Follow local style at all times. Find examples in the newspaper and include them in your stylebook.

In dealing with fractions, it is necessary to be aware that fractions may be expressed as percentages. For example, you may write "75%" instead of "three-fourths."

Furthermore, in writing percentages, as well as in general use, some papers prefer decimals to fractions: 8.5% instead of 8½% or 8.75 instead of 8-3/4.

A FINAL WORD

We have covered a lot of material in this chapter, but we have by no means covered all the details of newspaper style. It is hoped you now have a better understanding of what style is. Remain alert for peculiar usages.

Following style is the first step toward making your news releases more professional.

Probably the most difficult task at hand is compiling your own stylebook. It will be much easier if you make it a habit to clip examples of style when you see them, rather than trying to set up a complete stylebook in a single sitting. Once completed, however, I think you will find it a great help in removing much of the indecision about how certain material should be presented. Using the examples given in this chapter should help considerably.

If you must compile your own stylebook, I recommend that you keep carbon copies of your stories so that you can see what changes the editors have made in your articles. Any errors of style should be noted in your stylebook.

Cross-checking your copy with the article as it appears in print also will help you to identify other errors you may be making, many of which will be dealt with in the chapters to follow.

4

Policy

RAISON d'ETRE

Newspaper policies are often a source of dissension between editors and contributors. By and large, these policies establish what the paper will *not* print rather than what it will and it is, perhaps, this negative aspect of policy which is the cause for the dissension.

The reasons for various policies may range from some subjective basis, such as a publisher's personal philosophy, to more pragmatic considerations, such as the need to work within deadlines.

Whatever the reasons, editors already harried by the pressure of deadlines and exacerbated by sloppy news copy have neither the time nor the inclination to defend or explain the policies established by their newspapers.

It remains, then, for you to learn to work within the limits set by the policies which your local papers have established. If you feel a policy is unfair, I suggest that you state your objections in a polite letter to the managing editor. At no time should you argue with a subordinate editor who is trying to enforce the policies under which both you and he must work.

As indicated, a paper's policy may be based on a publisher's or editor's prejudices or attitudes. Many papers are either Republican or Democratic in inclination and it sometimes is difficult to get favorable treatment for the party the paper opposes. There are papers with "s-o-b" lists, persons and organizations who are not to receive favorable mention. On the other side, some papers cater to big advertisers and an advertiser's favorite organization will get better play than it deserves. If the publisher has strong feelings about consumer groups, for example, these groups can send in tons of press releases and see none printed. At the same time, his wife's social club may get front page notice with pictures. There's not much the newspaper staff can do about the situation and all you, as a contributor, can do is learn the paper's prejudices and try not to incur the displeasure of anyone on the paper.

Incidentally, to tell a reporter, "I know your publisher. He's a frequent guest at dinner" will not earn you his support. You're pulling rank on him and he won't like it.

Sometimes a newspaper will suggest its philosophy in a slogan carried with its nameplate or state policy in its masthead or elsewhere on its editorial page.

For example, the *Pottsville* (Pa.) *Republican* carries on its front page the following subtitle: "Schuylkill County's Newspaper." That slogan suggests an emphasis on local coverage.

Indeed, the Feb. 15, 1975, front page of the *Republican,* taken at random, carried five news stories. Each had a local orientation. The first was about a local fire. The second was about a Chamber of Commerce luncheon. The third was an Associated Press report about a state program affecting pharmacies, which ran with a story about local reaction to the program (the fourth story).

The fifth story was another Associated Press report, this one about a proposed tax on cars which do not get good gasoline mileage. Even the subject of that story would have a direct effect on the *Republican's* readers.

The implication of all this is that the *Republican* prefers stories which have local origin and/or local impact to broader, less local articles.

Newspapers exist to serve the readers in their circulation areas and therefore the emphasis is on news which occurs within those areas. It is rare these days for even the smallest town not to have available the editions of a large metropolitan newspaper which tries to cover the affairs of an entire state or even of a region of the nation. The smaller papers compete by intensive coverage of their local areas and therefore most are committed to a policy of stressing local affairs over the large national events which their readers will learn about from the larger newspapers and from radio and television.

On the other hand, the famous motto of the *New York Times,* "All the News That's Fit to Print," suggests much broader policy limits, which one would expect from a newspaper of its size and scope. Still, the word "fit" suggests that the *Times,* too, reserves the right to restrict or refuse to print stories which it deems "unfit" for publication.

There is a facetious version of the *Times'* motto: "All the News That Fits We Print." The jest suggests a space restriction.

Sometimes a newspaper will express its policy in more definitive terms. On its editorial page, the *Berwick* (Pa.) *Enterprise* carries the following notice to its readers:

Letters to the Editor will be published only if they are signed in ink, by the author. Name of the author will be published. Letters should be kept brief with a maximum

**of 300 words. Longer letters will be judged on content.
The Berwick Enterprise wishes to explain letters do not
reflect policy of the publication and makes no decision
on authenticity of the material submitted.**

Policies, of course, vary from paper to paper across
the country. Some papers, unlike the *Enterprise*, for
example, may require that letters to the editor be signed
but they promise to withhold the author's name upon
request.

Trying to account for all the policies of newspapers
across the United States, then, would be a task of enormous undertaking.

Instead, this chapter attempts to set forth some of
the more basic considerations upon which newspaper
policies, by and large, are likely to be established.

In so doing, it is hoped that the would-be news writer
will become more understanding of the reasons for establishing policy and will learn to work within the restrictions which are imposed by newspapers within his geo-
graphical location.

NEWS VALUE

Identifying the news value of any given story is
probably the most important judgment you will have to
make in writing a news article. You will have to recognize
news value to apply the information presented in Chapter 6, "The News Story," and "The Feature" in Chapter 7.

News value—the very essence of journalism—is a
difficult concept to define. Broadly speaking, news value
is what makes a person read a story.

The principal function of a news story is to provide
information. However, not all information will be of
interest to all people. It is the *quality* of the information,
then, which will determine the degree of news value one

story will have *on a given day, relative to other stories submitted on that same day.*

It is important to note this *relative* aspect of news value. Let us examine this important consideration more closely.

Suppose an editor has 10 stories. We will assign a value of "1" to the most important of those stories and a value of "10" to the least important. We have not yet discussed what makes a story "important," but we will deal with that shortly.

The story which has a news value of "1" will get the biggest headline for that day. The "10" story will get the smallest display.

On the next day, however, the story which received a "1" the day before may have a news value of "2" or "6," depending upon the importance of the other stories against which it is being judged.

For example, a train crash which kills five people may get top play on a day when nothing more important has happened. If that same train crash happens on a day when 100 people are killed in a plane crash, however, the plane crash will get top play. "Importance," in this case, is based upon the number of people killed.

Aware that news value is relative, then, let us return to the discussion of what decides the degree of quality of a piece of information, what makes it interesting, what determines its *news value.*

Generally speaking, the news value of a story will depend upon four basic considerations: uniqueness, freshness, importance to the reader, and where the event in the story took place. We will consider these elements in order.

Uniqueness. This is probably the most obvious element of news value. The more unusual an event is, the higher its news value is likely to be. The importance of this aspect of news value is dealt with again in Chapter 6.

Freshness. Newspapers want to publish stories about events as soon after the event occurs as possible. Not only that, papers strive to be first in reporting any given event. In journalism, the drive to "scoop" the opposition is innate. No matter how routine a story may be, its news value is greatest the first time it is published and diminishes with each subsequent report and with the elapse of time between the occurrence of an event and the date it is published. In writing a series of stories to publicize a single club event, you have to find a fresh approach to each story. That situation, too, is dealt with in Chapter 6.

Importance. The number of readers who will be affected by a story, directly and indirectly, and the weight of the impact of the story on those readers has a bearing on news value. The more people affected and the more serious the consequences of a story, the greater its news value. If you find an element within a story which will broaden its appeal among the readers of your local paper, move that element to the beginning of the story. Broadening the appeal of a story will be discussed again in Chapter 6.

Location. The last of these four elements may be the decisive factor in determining the story's importance. If that plane crash killing 100 people occurred in the paper's circulation area, it is the big news of the day. It's also big news if most of the passengers were from the local area even though the crash occurred a continent away. But in a small town, if two local residents were killed in an automobile smashup on the day of the plane crash, the traffic mishap will be the big news. (Readers can get the news about the plane crash from the metropolitan papers, radio or television.) Most of your stories will originate locally, but be alert for stories about former club members or other local people who are involved in newsworthy events outside the local area. What happens to these former local residents may still be news to your local paper.

These four elements of news value apply to the feature as well as the news story. One other element applies exclusively to the feature: emotional impact.

As will be discussed in Chapter 7, the feature employs a looser construction than the news story and is designed to evoke a tear or a smile or strike some other emotional chord within the reader. If you find that the information about a given event or a person within the story you are about to write evokes an emotional response, consider whether the story might not be better written as a feature, rather than as a straight news piece.

THE VALUE OF SPACE

At the root of many policy decisions is the need to use valuable newspaper space to the best advantage. Space limitations, for example, may be the reason for restricting the length of stories, for the taboo against multiple submissions, and for the stress on improving news value to elevate stories above the routine.

By limiting the length of your stories to no more than two pages (three if you triple space) your stories are far more likely to be tight and crisp and less boring to the reader.

If you absolutely need more space, the paper will give it to you, but some papers may impose arbitrary space limits on routine club releases. Perhaps the following illustration will help you to understand why.

News space is too valuable to be wasted. Ask any advertiser what it costs him for space in the newspaper and you are likely to be surprised.

Let us say that you write a several-page article which will take up 10 inches of space in the newspaper—a story two columns wide and five inches deep in each column. Map out a section of that size in your local paper. An advertiser buying that space from one newspaper in the area where I live would pay $3.36 per column inch—in other words, $33.60.

If you had to pay that kind of money to have your stories published, I am certain that you would trim them considerably.

It has been my experience, incidentally, that the less a person knows about his subject, the more words he needs to write about it.

MULTIPLE SUBMISSIONS

Editors, you will recall, all like to have the first break on stories. That, along with the value of news space, is why I advised in Chapter 2 not to send a story to more than one paper in your area, if that is the prevailing policy of the area's newspapers. Editors are assured that an "exclusive" will not be published first in a competing paper. If you were an editor, would you publish a second-hand story before a brand new one? By all means, work with all the papers in your area, but use only one at a time.

Some papers may include radio and television in this multiple submission prohibition; others may limit the restriction only to other newspapers.

Remember, though, never to submit a carbon or photo copy of a story. Editors regard a copy as a sign that a story is making the rounds and many will discard such stories immediately. (Also, carbons and photo copies often tend to illegibility.)

DUGAN'S DEFINITION

Tom Dugan, a colleague and a veteran of more than 40 years in the newspaper business, has coined a rule which he uses to categorize stories.

Dugan's Definition
   The first time a story appears in print it is news. The second time it appears, it is publicity. The third time it appears, it is advertising.

Newspapers prefer to have "news" as defined by Dugan. In addition, they often tolerate club stories which are really "publicity." Advertising is willingly accepted, too, but for that, there is a charge.

With regard to advertising, most newspapers have strict policies against stories which have a commercial angle or which quote fees or ticket prices. Usually, a decision is made by the advertising director and the managing editor on whether to run such stories as free news or paid advertising.

Check your local paper to see if it allows the quotation of ticket prices or other fees which may be connected with an event your club is sponsoring. Some papers prohibit such quotations. Other papers may allow the quotation of prices for events which they consider a "public service."

In fact, a paper may waive other policy restrictions where public service stories are involved. For example, if the volunteer fire company is distributing stickers to be placed on the windows of homes of invalids and children, a paper may waive its policy against multiple submissions. Do not, however, consistently break a story in one paper and expect its competition to perform the "public service." Take turns.

TELEPHONE NUMBERS

Some newspaper policies prohibit the publication of telephone numbers. The reason is a practical one. As I said earlier, typographical errors are difficult to control and the potential for such errors is extremely great in telephone numbers. Another reason for not publishing telephone numbers is to discourage crank calls.

In addition to being absolutely worthless if even one digit is wrong, incorrect telephone numbers mean that someone other than the intended party will be receiving calls having to do with something he knows nothing about, which can be extremely irritating.

Most newspapers make an exception for emergency numbers like police, fire and ambulance services. An extra effort will be required to ensure that no error has been made and the newspaper feels it is impractical to expend that effort except for these emergency numbers and in paid advertising space.

There is a solution, however, if you are dealing with a newspaper whose policy prohibits telephone numbers. Instead of writing the number, give the name of the individual or organization exactly as it appears in the telephone directory. That way, the reader will be able to look up the number for himself.

DEADLINES

Another policy which has a practical basis is the requirement that stories be submitted by a certain time in order to be considered for publication in a given edition. The time specified is, of course, known as the *deadline,* a term with which you should be familiar.

Each news story must be processed through a series of steps before getting into print. These steps will be outlined in Chapter 9. Each step requires time and the deadline ensures that the time is available. In addition, a newspaper may have several deadlines which apply to its various sections to control the flow of news stories and typesetting. A weekly paper, for example, may have a mid-week deadline for its feature section, while the deadline for page one is the last possible moment before the press run. The paper, in other words, is closed down in stages.

All newspapers have deadlines and it is up to you to check with your local paper to find out what its deadlines are. If you file a story by mail, be sure to mail it early enough to meet the specified deadline.

And remember, if you miss a deadline, it is your fault and not the paper's.

LETTERS TO THE EDITOR

Newspapers take great pains to ensure that news stories are objective and unbiased. In the next chapter, you will learn how to handle subjective comment through the use of the direct and indirect quotation.

You may find, however, that a situation having to do with your organization requires subjective comment. Perhaps you feel that the public is not giving your organization the support it needs to conduct certain public service programs. You and the other members of your organization sacrifice personal time to work on volunteer projects of benefit to the community-at-large and are miffed by public apathy.

Every newspaper allows space for comment by its readers. Instead of trying to write a news story about the situation, consider venting your feelings in a "letter to the editor."

You have a great deal of freedom in letters to the editor, so long as you do not write anything which is in bad taste or potentially libelous.

Some papers, like the *Berwick Enterprise,* which was mentioned earlier in this chapter, require that letters to the editor be signed. Others will withhold the name of the author from publication upon request.

PICTURES

No doubt, you will have occasion to use pictures with stories from time to time. Usually, newspapers have rules which apply to the use of photographs. There are guides, for example, on picture quality and how identifications are to be written.

In addition, newspapers prefer action pictures to static shots which show a group of people lined up in rows.

A newspaper also may restrict certain categories of pictures—shots of children celebrating birthdays, for example—because they are too routine, and if the paper publishes one, it has to explain to proud parents why it won't publish all the others.

Chapter 8 is devoted entirely to the subject of pictures.

LIVING WITH POLICY

Your job as publicity chairman will be much more enjoyable if you develop a rapport with your local editors. You do not develop this rapport by arguing over the unfairness of various policies.

As I suggested at the beginning of this chapter, if you feel a policy is unfair, write a letter to the managing editor. You will find his name in the paper's masthead on the editorial page. A polite letter will get a better reception than an angry one.

Another source of misunderstanding comes from persons other than yourself submitting news releases to the papers. To guard against multiple submissions and duplication in the same paper, either of which may occur without your knowledge and get you into hot water with the editor, ask your club president to make it clear to the members that you are the only one authorized to submit news releases on behalf of the organization.

Studying your local paper will help you develop a feel for the kinds of stories it uses. It may be useful to include a policy section in your stylebook.

All newspapers need news and contributing writers like yourself are a valuable extension of the professional staff. That value is diminished, however, if you ignore style and policy. Keep this in mind as you proceed through the rest of this book.

5

Grammar

THE SOUND OF NEWS

The English language: Full of gerunds, appositives, past perfect tenses and subjunctive moods, is it any wonder that even the best of us frequently use an objective case pronoun when the nominative is called for, or split an occasional infinitive, or dangle a participle now and then?

Much has been written, recently, in trade journals and magazines about the deterioration of grammar and spelling. The criticisms are made not only of non-professional writers and of students coming out of journalism schools, but of professional writers as well.

Newspaper editors groan over errors in noun-verb agreement and misplaced apostrophes in possessive nouns and wonder aloud if grammar still is being taught in the nation's schools.

In light of the number of books written on grammar

and the years devoted to the subject in school, this one chapter could not hope to cover all the errors of which non-professionals and professionals alike are guilty.

I strongly recommend that you visit a book store and pick up any of the many excellent grammar reviews which are available.

Two books, both paperbacks, which I keep on my reference shelf, are: *Questions You Always Wanted to Ask About English* by Maxwell Nurnberg and *The Most Common Mistakes in English Usage* by Thomas Elliott Berry.

I also recommend Edwin Newman's *Strictly Speaking,* a brief and entertaining look at the language and how it is used and abused, in which Newman poses the question: "Will America be the death of English?"

This chapter does not intend to quarrel over fine points. I like what Norman Lewis says in his book *Word Power Made Easy.*

The purist is a hidebound reactionary who wishes to keep the English language in a strait jacket despite preponderant and unmistakable evidence that English is always changing, that grammar is constantly tending to loosen up and become more liberal, and that popular deviations from old-fashioned rules freshen and invigorate American speech.

Still, we cannot allow the language to become so loose that good ideas are lost in ambiguity and *communication* becomes ever more difficult to achieve.

Communication is the goal of journalism. Whether it is the time and place of a PTA meeting or an important community project to be undertaken, the news story communicates information to the reader.

In my opinion, this information is best conveyed through simple, direct sentences which say what must be said in as few words as possible and without any danger of confusion.

This chapter, then, will deal with some of the more common faults of non-professionals—faults which encumber writing with superfluous words and rambling sentences—and common errors which are easily recognized and corrected.

THE PASSIVE VOICE

The passive voice is a legitimate grammatical form, but in news writing its use tends to make sentences longer than they need to be and delays the reader in getting to the point.

In news writing, it is well to keep in mind those contests which ask you to say something "in 25 words or less." Your goal should be simplicity and directness.

As an illustration, let us suppose that you want to announce a meeting of the PTA.

We may announce the meeting using the passive voice, or we may use the active voice:

Example 1
Passive: A meeting of the PTA *will be held* **on Tuesday night at 8.**
Active: The PTA *will meet* **on Tuesday night at 8.**

Notice how much shorter and more direct the active voice is. The passive requires three words for the verb, while the active requires only two. In addition, the passive construction requires a subject of five words, where two suffice in the active.

It is this kind of economy of words which we are after.

But brevity is not the sole objection to the passive construction. Active verbs are more dynamic than passive ones; they have more punch. Dynamic words will make stories more interesting and, therefore, more likely to be read than dull ones.

Active constructions are more dynamic and stronger for a reason. In the active voice, the subject is performing some action through the verb. The subject is *acting*. In the passive voice, the subject is being *acted upon*. Something is being done to it. The subject is submitting.

Make an effort to eliminate the passive voice from your writing wherever possible. In Example 2, I provide several illustrations of the active and passive voice.

Example 2
　　Passive: Officers *will be elected* by VFW Post 123 tomorrow night at 8.
　　Active: VFW Post 123 *will elect* officers tomorrow night at 8.
　　Passive: A meeting of the PTA *was held* last night.
　　Active: The PTA *met* last night.

The appearance of the word "be" or some other helping verb—"was" and "were," for example—indicates that you are using the passive voice.

THE FALSE PASSIVE

Even though it should be avoided, the passive voice is a legitimate grammatical construction. The *false passive* is not.

Objections to the false passive may seem like quibbling, but it is covered in journalism texts and editors who are trying to arrest the decay of grammar will eliminate it. Correcting the false passive is annoying to editors because it requires reconstructing the entire sentence, as opposed to a simple word addition, deletion or substitution.

Grammatical analysis of the false passive is complex and is left to books on grammar. It is necessary only to recognize that the false passive usually occurs when someone *receives* something, such as an award or a commendation. "Receives" is the key word. When someone receives something, say he *received* it.

Example 3
The PTA officers *received* awards for service.

If the false passive were used, that statement would read: "The PTA officers *were given* awards for service." The meaning may be clear, but the construction is ungrammatical. Follow Example 3 and use "received" when this situation arises.

OTHER ERRORS

An error prevalent among professional as well as novice news writers is the mistaking of collective nouns as plural (council, club, board, association, class, etc.).

Collective nouns do represent numbers of people, but in American usage they are singular in construction with pronouns and verbs. For example:

> **Not: The council voted 6-0. *They* argued. . . .**
> **But: The council voted 6-0. *It* argued. . . .**
> **Not: The Franklin PTA will show *their* colors at the spring fashion show.**
> **But: The Franklin PTA will show *its* colors at the spring fashion show. Or make it the PTA *members* will show *their* colors. . . .**

Placement of the apostrophe in possessives is another problem. For example, "its" is possessive and "it's" is a contraction for "it is." Singular possessives, such as "council's decision," are formed by adding "'s." Plural possessives add the apostrophe after the "s": "The teachers' salaries. . . ."

Singular nouns ending in "s" add only the apostrophe: "Jones' position was. . . ." (Note: "Jones's" is not incorrect and some paper's may require " 's" under the rules of style.)

COMBINING IDEAS

In Example 2, the active voice eliminated helping verbs and prepositions. In many cases, prepositional phrases can be eliminated in favor of one-word adjectives, further condensing a sentence.

Example 4
A meeting of the PTA of the Franklin Elementary School of Anytown will be held on Tuesday night at 8.

By converting to the active voice and substituting one-word adjectives for prepositional phrases, we produce the following sentence, which contains the same information but is more succinct.

Example 5
The Anytown Franklin Elementary School PTA will meet on Tuesday night at 8.

Often, publicity chairmen will spread related ideas over two sentences, when it is better to combine the ideas in a single sentence.

Example 6
The Franklin Elementary PTA will hold a meeting on Tuesday night at 8. The purpose of the meeting will be to make plans for a rummage sale.

Two pieces of information are provided in Example 6: The PTA will meet and a rummage sale will be planned. One way of combining this information in a single sentence is illustrated in the following example.

Example 7
The Franklin Elementary PTA will plan a rummage sale at a meeting on Tuesday night at 8.

We have substituted a single sentence of 17 words for two sentences which totalled 27 words.

It is important to notice the elimination of the words "hold" and "make" from Example 6. Nonprofessionals tend to inflate the language. Why say "will hold a meeting" when you can say "will meet," and "will make plans" when you can say "will plan"?

Remember: The goal is to try to trim all the fat from the language.

ADJECTIVES AND ADVERBS

Adjectives modify nouns and pronouns and adverbs modify verbs, adjectives and other adverbs. In "Franklin Elementary PTA," *Franklin Elementary* tells the reader which PTA you are writing about. In "He worked quickly," *quickly* describes how the work was performed.

Adjectives and adverbs should be used with caution in news writing because they can be enemies of objectivity. The reason is that they usually require subjective judgments.

To say that the Empire State Building is "tall" will go without objection, but to say that it is "beautiful" injects a subjective judgment which certainly will be challenged by someone who finds the building "ugly."

If you describe the food at a firemen's bazaar as "delicious," someone else might find it too bland or too spicy.

In short, avoid the use of modifiers when they involve subjective judgments. What you consider to be an "interesting" lecture might have been "boring" to someone else.

DIRECT QUOTATIONS

The late Thomas E. Heffernan, editor and publisher of the Wilkes-Barre, Pa., *Sunday Independent* from

1951 to 1970, held as his journalistic credo: "No friends to favor; no enemies to punish."

That motto is an admirable one and states very well one of the principal tenets of journalism: *objectivity*.

Non-professionals seem to find it difficult to stand back and judge their stories with objective detachment. The reason, perhaps, is that they are so deeply involved with the programs and projects of their particular clubs and organizations.

Still, the need arises to express opinions and subjective comments and the would-be reporter must learn to present such views without damaging the newspaper's objectivity.

There are places within the newspaper which are reserved for subjective comment—letters to the editor, for example. Columnists, too, express opinions in commentaries published under their bylines. Subjective comment also is made, of course, in newspaper editorials. In all these cases, the reader knows he is reading the *opinions* of one person.

Making subjective comment in news stories, on the other hand, is a breach of journalistic principles known as *editorializing*.

To maintain objectivity, news stories are written in the third person, which keeps the writer from intruding, and all subjective comment must be attributed to a source other than the paper. A source can be quoted directly or indirectly and he may remain anonymous, if he wishes, by being referred to as a "spokesman," an "official," a "source," or some similar designation.

Adjectives and adverbs are a threat to objectivity.

If a news story says that afghans made as prizes for the church social are "beautiful," that remark must be attributed to some source. Otherwise, the remark is automatically attributed to the newspaper and the paper is guilty of editorializing.

Suppose that you are preparing a story about the church social and you want to write about the "beautiful" afghans which will be offered as door prizes. You can attribute the subjective comment about the beauty of the afghans to the president of the organization which is sponsoring the social. Consider the following example.

Example 8
The Confraternity of Christian Mothers will hold its annual social on Saturday afternoon at 2 in St. Mary's Church.

"Beautiful handmade afghans will again be offered as door prizes," said President Jane Doe, who also reminded patrons that "delicious Lithuanian foods will be served at the traditional buffet supper."

In addition to protecting the newspaper's objectivity by attributing subjective comments to an outside source, direct quotations also function like salt and pepper to add zest and seasoning to a story by breaking up the narrative.

But the direct quotation has still another function which contributes to its importance as a journalistic device.

No doubt, your club will have occasion to invite guest speakers to lecture on some topic of interest to club members. Naturally, you expect the speaker to have some expertise about his subject.

You would expect, for example, that a speaker who plans to discuss the plight of education in an address to the PTA will have some experience in the field of education. Otherwise, his opinions and comments may carry no more weight than yours or anyone else's.

This additional function of the direct quotation, then, is to attribute statements to some authority.

One of the officers of your club may be the authority to which certain remarks are attributed. Most club presidents like to have their names in the paper and, indeed, they are deserving of such recognition for their willingness to assume club responsibilities on a volunteer basis.

Most publicity chairmen recognize their presidents by writing things like "President John Doe presided." We have already noted the objection that such remarks are superfluous. Why not, then, let the club president say something substantial?

For example, many publicity chairmen in the area where I live end stories about club meetings which are coming up with the following sentence: "All members are urged to attend."

Without attributing such statements to some authority, the newspaper, as we have seen, takes the responsibility for the statement. In most cases, the newspaper does not care one way or another whether club members attend a meeting, nor does it have any responsibility for "urging" them to do so.

If the president of your club has noticed a problem of absenteeism, you have a ready-made situation for a direct quote. If you quote the president in a way similar to the following example, you maintain the paper's objectivity by attributing the remark to a specific authority.

Example 9
President John Doe said, "I urge all members to attend this meeting. Only through the full participation of the membership can the PTA continue to provide service to the city's schools."

It is not always necessary to quote an authority directly. You can paraphrase remarks in an indirect quotation, as I do in the following example. Notice the absence of quotation marks. Quotation marks are used only when you are using the *exact* words of the person being quoted.

Example 10
In urging all members of the PTA to attend this meeting, President John Doe said that absenteeism

is beginning to interfere with the operation of the organization.

I have devoted a lot of space to the direct quotation because it is an important journalistic device. You are encouraged to use direct quotes frequently in your writing, and, for that reason, you must know how to punctuate quoted matter.

PUNCTUATING QUOTATIONS

For most non-professionals—and even some professional writers—where to place commas and periods in relation to the quotation marks presents an annoying problem.

The solution is simple: Periods and commas which follow quoted matter always are placed within the quotation marks. That is true for book titles as well as quoted statements.

If a comma precedes a quote, it is placed outside the quotation marks.

The placement of a question mark will depend upon the context of the sentence. If an interrogative sentence ends with a quote which does not ask a question, the question mark will be placed outside the quotation marks. If a declarative sentence ends with an interrogative quotation, the question mark will be placed inside the quotation marks.

The placement of question marks, commas and other marks of punctuation are illustrated in the following example.

Example 11
    Concluding comma: "I agree," he said.
    Preceding comma: He said, "I agree."
    Period: The book club will discuss "Gone With the Wind." (No comma is needed before a single book title.)
    Semicolon: The book club will discuss "Gone With

the Wind"; however, more modern works are on the agenda.

Exclamation point: "Out!" the sergeant-at-arms shouted.

Question mark: Will the membership respond to the president's request for "better attendance"? (Interrogative sentence ending with a quote which does not ask a question.)

Question mark: The president asked, "Are all members here?" (Declarative sentence which ends with an interrogative quote.)

Titles in series: The book club will discuss "Gone With the Wind," "War and Peace" and "Herzog." (Note placement of comma and period.)

It is a good idea for you to study the previous example until you are thoroughly familiar with the placement of punctuation in relation to quotation marks. Other problems of punctuation will be dealt with later in this chapter.

THE THIRD PERSON

Objectivity in news writing also is maintained by writing from the point of view of the *third person*. In the third person, the writer does not intrude upon his article or whatever else he is writing, as I do when I use the first person "I" or the second person "you" in this book, for example.

Because the third person is detached from the story, it is more objective than either the first person or second person.

Only in direct quotations, editorials, letters to the editor and columns—all of which are open to subjective comment—will anything but the third person be used.

For example, I am sure you are familiar with the editorial "we," which is the first person plural. In its editorials, a newspaper refers to itself as "we." Likewise, a columnist may refer to himself through the editorial "we" or simply as "I," the first person singular.

In the news story, however, you will never refer to yourself in the narrative, nor will you quote yourself as the writer of the article. Nor will you use the second person to direct your story to one or more specific individuals. One part-time correspondent for my paper is fond of phrases like "We need your help," for example. You should never intrude like that. Such phrases may be used if they are quoted and attributed to someone within the organization: "We need your help," the PTA president said.

Similarly, never use first person possessive pronouns. For example, refer to a ruling by the PTA as the "PTA's position," and not as "our position."

THE PRESENT PERFECT TENSE

Obviously, stories about past events will be written in the past tense and stories about future stories will be written in the future tense.

But, some club publicity chairmen have a tendency to use the *present perfect tense* in place of the past tense.

The present perfect tense is used to describe action which began in the past and is continuing in the present, while the past tense describes action which is over and done with.

It is common, for example, to find: "PTA President John Doe *has* announced that. . . ."

The announcement was made at some time in the past. Although the effects of the announcement may carry forward to the present and beyond, the actual act of "announcing" is over and done with. The writer should have used the simple past tense: PTA President John Doe announced that. . . ."

Like the passive voice, the present perfect tense is a

legitimate grammatical form. It should be used only when appropriate, however, as is the case in writing about a drive to collect aluminum cans which is still going on at the time the story is published.

You might write, for example: "To date, the Lions Club *has* collected over 200 aluminum cans in a program which will raise money for club projects and help to clean up Anytown in the bargain."

Occasionally, I have found some publicity chairmen who use the present tense inappropriately.

Newspapers cannot report events as they are happening, unlike radio and television, which can air reports direct from the scene of a meeting or a fire.

Because of the time required to process news, papers carry stories about events which have already happened or are going to happen.

In stating a position of your particular club on some issue, the present tense may be appropriate to establish that the position is one currently held by the club.

The present tense is justified in the following sentence: "The PTA is opposed to a tax increase," which expresses the present position of the PTA. Similarly, the PTA president may express his *present* opinion: "The president *feels* a tax increase is not justified."

I often find publicity chairmen using the present tense to describe a past event: "President John Doe *says* the members are to be congratulated." Use "said" not "says."

Newspapers do use the present tense in headlines to denote past time in order to give stories a sense of immediacy. But headlines are a special case and rules used for them do not apply elsewhere.

PUNCTUATION

One of the most troublesome punctuation marks is the comma. We already have seen how it is used in a direct quotation.

A problem arises when commas occur in pairs. Often the second comma is forgotten.

Appositives, which identify nouns, are set off by pairs of commas: "John Doe, *the committee chairman*, gave his report." Many non-professionals omit the second comma.

Relative clauses also require pairs of commas: "John Doe, *who is the committee chairman*, gave his report."

Likewise, parenthetical remarks require pairs of commas: "The president, *of course*, will continue to preside at the meetings."

Comma pairs also set off the year in a date and the name of a state when it is used with the name of a city or town:

> **"Oct. 1, *1975*, was the date. . . ."**
> **"Boston, *Mass.*, is a city. . . ."**

Situations involving appositives, relative clauses and parenthetical remarks, in which comma pairs are needed (and *essential* clauses, which require no commas), are not always easy to identify. I strongly recommend that you study the use of commas in an English grammar text.

The comma splice is another error involving the comma. It occurs when a comma incorrectly is used to connect two independent sentences: "Absenteeism is becoming a serious problem, it will be discussed at the next meeting."

A conjunction or a semicolon must be used to connect those two independent sentences or they must be separated entirely. A comma will not do:

> **"Absenteeism is becoming a serious problem and it will be discussed at the next meeting."**
>
> **or**
>
> **"Absenteeism is becoming a serious problem; it will be discussed at the next meeting."**
>
> **or**
>
> **"Absenteeism is becoming a serious problem. It will be discussed at the next meeting."**

A semicolon may be used in place of a conjunction or as a strong comma when two independent ideas are closely related. In addition, the semicolon is used with the comma in some cases to separate words in a series.

Consider the following example, in which the results of a club election are reported.

Example 12
The Franklin Elementary PTA last night elected the following officers: Jane Doe, president; Thomas Smith, vice president; John Doe, secretary; and Edward Jenkins, treasurer.

In Example 12, it is clear who was elected to which office, but it is not uncommon to find listings like the following: "Jane Doe, president, Thomas Smith, vice president, secretary, John Doe, and Edward Jenkins, treasurer"; or, worse, "president Jane Doe, vice president; Thomas Smith, secretary, John Doe, treasurer, Edward Jenkins."

An outrageous example to emphasize a point? Not so. I actually have edited stories containing such gobbledygook and it is that kind of ignorance or indifference which sours editors' dispositions.

There are a few things to keep in mind when dealing with a complicated series of words.

First of all, the comma and semicolon are not interchangeable. Everything within the semicolons in Example 12 is related. Commas are used within the semicolons to separate a secondary series.

In the illustration which follows Example 12, notice the confusion which is caused by the careless use of commas and semicolons. The reader must wade through the series to be sure which person holds which office.

An editor, of course, cannot allow such confusion to appear in print. He must grudgingly put the words in order or throw the piece away. Many editors will choose the latter alternative.

For one thing, the semicolon after "vice president," above, separated the office from its holder, Thomas Smith. Furthermore, there is no consistency of style in presenting the officers' names and their titles.

In Example 12, the style I used lists the officer's name followed by his title. That style is maintained throughout. I did not switch halfway through to title followed by name. Notice, too, how the words within the semicolons are related.

I recommend the style presented in Example 12 for use whenever you are required to list a similar series of words.

For example, you have to list a series of committees and committee chairmen. First, list the name of the committee, followed by a comma, then the names of the members of the committee, each separated by a comma, then the word "and" followed by the chairman's name, another comma, and the word "chairman," followed by a semicolon. After the semicolon, begin with the name of the next committee and repeat the process.

Usually, long lists of committees will be broken up into paragraphs, even though a list of names does not form a complete sentence. Example 13 illustrates a common style which incorporates the suggestions just made.

Example 13
PTA Chairman John Doe last night appointed the following standing committees:

Tickets, John Doe, Jane Doe, Agnes Smith and Edward Jenkins, chairman; hospitality, George Edwards, Mary Jones and William Thomas, chairman.

Ways and means, Donald Riley, Ruth Johnson and Robert Donner, chairman; entertainment, Samuel Barnes, Joseph Richards and David Roberts, chairman.

You may find, of course, that some newspapers have a policy which prohibits such listings altogether. Others may list committee members but not their respective titles or the names of the committees, usually because one member might be on several committees and the repetition of the same name in several places is considered a waste of space.

Sometimes, dashes may be used to list a series of items. If the president of a club is issuing a list of policy statements, you could use a style like that presented in the following example.

Example 14
PTA President John Doe last night made the following policy statements:
—He is opposed to an increase in the schools tax rate.
—He will seek more participation by fathers in club activities.
—He supports club endorsement of school board candidates.

In cases similar to Example 12 and Example 13, however, never use dashes (except as indicated in the above example), asterisks, ellipses (a series of dots usually used to indicate an omission in a direct quotation), a succession of blank spaces (as I have found on occasion), or any mark or symbol except commas and semicolons.

In a simple series of words, of course, only commas are required to separate the elements which comprise the series: "PTA members elected a president, vice president, secretary and treasurer." Do not use semicolons to separate the words in simple series.

DO NOT OVERSIMPLIFY

One of the things I have stressed in news writing is simplicity. Parts of this chapter, for example, are devoted to ways in which you can make your writing more succinct, more direct. We will deal with simplicity again in the next chapter.

Simplicity, however, does not mean that you write in

what I call the "flyer" style. Flyers, as you know, list a number of facts about an event, one fact immediately after another, usually with little or no narrative. The writer merely itemizes his information.

An illustration of the flyer style is presented in the following example.

Example 15
Come one, come all!
Big rummage sale sponsored by the Franklin Elementary PTA
When—On Saturday afternoon at 2.
Where—In the Franklin School playground.
Help us to raise money to buy new encyclopedias for the school library.

That is carrying compactness a bit too far. Information presented in such a manner is acceptable in an advertisement, but it will never get into print as a news story.

If an editor is gracious enough, and can find someone on the staff who has time to put the story together for you, you will be most fortunate. It is more likely that this type of release will wind up in the trash basket.

CAPITALIZATION

Deciding what words to capitalize can be another problem for non-professionals unfamiliar with journalistic style.

Everyone knows that names of persons or schools or organizations, for example, are to be capitalized. The reason is that they are proper nouns; that is, they are *specific* persons, places or things. All other nouns are *common nouns* and are not capitalized, except, of course at the beginning of a sentence.

The problem arises, I suspect, because publicity

chairmen and others so strongly identify with their particular organizations that designations like "club" or "association" take on added importance. The same might be said of the various projects which are sponsored by the club.

Thus, an editor is likely to find a PTA publicity chairman referring to "the School" or "the Association," or a scoutmaster writing about his "Scouts." Each of these words, when it stands alone, is a common noun and should not be capitalized.

If you are writing about the Anytown Rotary Club, capitals are in order. Afterward, when you refer to "the club," lower case letters are in order.

Likewise, common nouns like "bake sale" and "rummage sale" should be capitalized only when they are part of a proper noun: "The Great Northeast Rummage Sale," for example. If you are writing: "The PTA will hold a *rummage sale* on Saturday," lower case is correct.

Titles also present a problem. When professional or official titles are written in front of a person's name, they are capitalized. If the title follows the name, it is no longer a title and is written in lower case. Thus, you would have "President John Doe," but "John Doe, president" or "Mayor John Doe," but "John Doe, mayor."

These nouns standing alone also are written in the lower case. You would write "the president of the PTA" or "the mayor said," for example. However, "president" sometimes is capitalized in references to the President of the United States: "The Franklin PTA will support the President's plan for higher education."

Titles of authority also follow the before and after rule for capitalization. Your club, for example, is likely to have a number of committees under the authority of a chairman. Write: "Chairman John Doe" or "John Doe, chairman."

In discussing capitalization, "false titles" should not

be capitalized, even when they precede a person's name. For example, in writing about delegates to a PTA convention, you would write: "According to *delegate* John Doe. . . ." or "John Doe, *delegate* to the PTA convention. . . ."

Committee names, when they are used with the name of the organization under which they function, should be capitalized, but they must be written in lower case when they stand alone. Thus: "The Franklin PTA Membership Committee" but "the membership committee" when it stands alone.

Branches of the United States armed forces usually are capitalized even when they are not preceded by "U.S.": Army, Navy, Marines, Air Force, Coast Guard, National Guard.

Local style may require that you disregard normal rules for capitalization. For example, the paper for which I work requires the word "courthouse" to be written as two words and capitalized: "Court House." You may find that other rules of grammar and spelling are modified by local style. Once again, local style will prevail and examples should be noted in your stylebook.

SPELLING

As an editor, I have given up expecting to find stories in which all words are spelled correctly. Almost everyone forgets the second "m" in "accommodate." And, if you remember to write "under way" as two words, you will be right more often than you will be wrong.

Spelling errors are not limited to non-professionals. One reporter I know always guesses wrong when choosing between "-ence" and "-ance" endings. Another consistently misspells "environment" as "enviornment." Both add an extra "l" to "marshal," which makes the word a proper name.

HYPHENATED WORDS

Compound adjectives which require hyphens can be troublesome. In the sentence, "The hike was 10 miles long," *10 miles long* is a predicate adjective separated from the noun it modifies (hike) by a linking verb (was). No hyphens are required. If, however, the adjective is placed in front of the noun, a hyphen is needed; thus: "A *10-mile* hike was held."

Similarly, if "a trophy is *four feet* high," it is a "*four-foot* trophy"; if "a girl is 10 years old," she is a "10-year-old girl." Many writers forget the second hyphen, between "year" and "old."

Omitting a hyphen can change the meaning of some words. For example, a "great grandfather" is a grandfather who is "great," but a "great-grandfather" is your grandfather's father.

Some papers eliminate the hyphen in some words as long as the meaning remains clear. Thus, one finds "cochairman" instead of "co-chairman" but "co-worker" instead of "coworker." Check style.

As a rule of thumb, you only need a hyphen for certain prefixes: "all-" as in "all-star"; "ex-" as in "ex-champion"; and "self-" as in "self-defense."

BEFORE GOING ON

Obviously, there has been much which has not been covered in this chapter. I have tried to deal with common errors and situations which have a particular bearing on news writing.

Here are the main points:
—Use the active voice rather than the passive for stronger, more compact writing; and beware of the false passive.
—Learn to combine ideas.

—Avoid subjective modifiers.

—Use direct quotations to season your writing and to maintain objectivity.

—Write in the third person and use the simple past tense and future tense.

—Use the comma and semicolon properly in a consistent style when presenting a series.

—Write briefly but do not oversimplify.

—Capitalize only proper nouns or when style requires.

There are other topics I might have covered: noun-verb agreement or redundancies.

Because I may have raised questions about grammar and because there is more to the subject than the scope of this book allows, I hope you will follow my suggestion to buy an English review book.

By learning to use the language properly, you will be able to communicate more effectively.

6

The News Story

A PROSE FORM

The news story is as distinct a prose form as the essay, the short story or the novel. As such, it has characteristics which set it apart from other prose forms.

Some of these characteristics already have been dealt with; for example, the use of active verbs instead of passive ones and the use of one-word adjectives instead of prepositional phrases for the sake of word economy.

In addition, following local style, which was discussed in Chapter 3, will give your stories a more professional sound and the format suggested in Chapter 2 will give them a more professional appearance.

But the use of the language is most important in making the news story a distinct prose form. The following suggestions will help you achieve that distinction:

—Use short, familiar words instead of long, difficult words.

—Use simple sentences in short paragraphs.
—Approach stories from a positive point of view, even when the story is about something negative.
—Eliminate all words, sentences or paragraphs which are redundant or superfluous.
—While common language is preferred, jargon and colloquialisms should not be used.

THE DIFFICULTY OF SIMPLICITY

A good news story will communicate information to the members of your organization and the public-at-large as simply and as straightforwardly as possible.

You might think of the news story as a piece of meat from which all the fat has been trimmed. Many people, in reading a newspaper, bite off chunks of information from the headlines or the first two or three paragraphs. For that reason, the information you are presenting must be in a form which is easily digested.

Learning to write simply is probably the most difficult thing for a beginning news writer to learn.

There is little room for creativity within the prose structure of the news story. You must learn to recognize the single most important piece of information and then to communicate that information as quickly and as clearly as possible.

GET TO THE POINT

In the news story, you must get to the point of the article at once. There are times when news stories—those of staff reporters and outside contributors alike—must be shortened to fit the space available. The editor will determine which paragraphs can be eliminated and order those paragraphs "killed."

News stories must be written so they may be "killed

from the bottom up," which means that the last two or three paragraphs may be discarded without eliminating any important facts. Killing from the bottom up expedites editing in the face of deadlines.

To cope with kill situations, then, you must learn to report your facts in order of importance, which will give your stories a triangular configuration. The most important piece of information will be at the apex of your "news triangle" and less important facts will expand gradually toward the base.

Exceptions to the "kill from the bottom up" style of editing occur mainly in the feature story, which will be discussed in the next chapter.

THE LEAD AND THE BODY

It will help you to think of a news story as being divided into two parts: the *lead* (pronounced "leed" and sometimes spelled that way) and the *body*.

The lead contains the single most important piece of information you wish to impart. *The lead in a news story always should be the first paragraph*. The body, on the other hand, contains information which develops the lead. It begins with the second paragraph and includes all subsequent paragraphs. If this rule is followed, the news story will have a triangular configuration, as illustrated in Figure 1.

Figure 1

```
        X            the lead
       XXX
      XXXXX
     XXXXXXX          the body
    XXXXXXXXX
   XXXXXXXXXXX
```

A reporter may complain that an editor has written a headline which misses the point of a story or that a dull headline has been written for a story which the reporter considers "important." Usually these complaints result from the reporter's error in not providing the material for the headline in his lead paragraph.

Copy editors are not infallible, but I have found it to be generally true that weak headlines come from weak leads and, conversely, that strong leads are conducive to strong headlines.

INTERROGATIVE LEADS

The purpose of a news story is to inform. If that is true, it follows that a story should never begin with a question. As far as I am concerned, a news story should answer questions, not ask them. Consider the following example:

Example 1
Will the Franklin Elementary PTA disband? That question will be answered tomorrow night at a special meeting in the school cafeteria.
PTA President Jane Doe said that the fate of the organization will depend upon how many members attend that meeting.

Any news story that can be started with an interrogative lead can just as easily be approached from a more positive angle, as Example 2 illustrates:

Example 2
The fate of the Franklin Elementary PTA will be decided at a special meeting tomorrow night at 8 in the school cafeteria.
Absenteeism has rendered the organization "ineffective," according to PTA President Jane Doe, who said that poor attendance at tomorrow night's meeting will result in "the immediate disbanding of the organization."

Sometimes, an interrogative lead can be remedied by simply eliminating the question part of the sentence.

Example 3
Interrogative: Did you know that the Franklin Elementary PTA provided more than $10,000 worth of equipment to the Anytown School District last year?

Declarative: The Franklin Elementary PTA provided more than $10,000 worth of equipment to the Anytown School District last year. (I simply omitted "did you know that" from the beginning of the sentence.)

There is no reason to play "Twenty Questions" with the reader. I view the interrogative lead as a sign of an amateur. Even in professional hands the interrogative lead and the interrogative headline should be used sparingly.

There is no need to ask a question which will be answered immediately. Furthermore, you ought to be thinking in terms of *answering* questions, not *asking* them.

THE FIVE W's

It is all well and good to talk about "leads" but how do you as a non-professional go about identifying the lead element from a jumble of disconnected facts?

Recognizing the lead element of a story can be a difficult problem for beginners. Most want to begin with what happened first and proceed chronologically to the end of the story, much as a club secretary prepares the minutes of a meeting. But, you are not the club secretary, you are the publicity writer.

If the most important item of business at a meeting occurs fifth on the agendum, the secretary will position that item chronologically within the minutes, but you, as publicity chairman, must learn to recognize important items and deal with them in order of importance. If you deal with an important item in the middle of your story, chances are the reader will no longer be with you by that time. You must "hook" him at once with a strong lead.

There are five basic questions which every novice news writer learns to ask which help him to categorize his facts and make the job of selecting a lead element easier.

Those five questions are known collectively as *The Five W's*. They are: *who, what, when, where* and *why* (or *how*).

The Five W's are the basic building blocks of any news story and it is with them that the news triangle is constructed.

Another important function of the Five W's is to ensure that none of the essential facts has been left out of the story. Let us examine how the Five W's might be used to prepare a simple meeting announcement:

Example 4
　　The Franklin Elementary PTA (who) will meet (what) on Tuesday night at 8 (when) in the school cafeteria (where) to plan a rummage sale (why).

Example 4 would not be a good story lead, but it does help to illustrate how the Five W's are used. Organizations often use "notices" like Example 4 to announce meetings; in these announcements, the lead and the body are combined in a single paragraph.

Journalism used to require that the essential Five W's of the news story be included in the lead paragraph. That is no longer true. The idea now is to pick out the single most important fact—the most important "W"— and include other information but making sure the paragraph does not become too lengthy.

What you should notice in Example 4 are some of the principles we already have dealt with. Notice the use of the active "will meet" instead of the passive "meeting will be held." Redundancies like "Tuesday *night* at 8 P.M."

were avoided. One-word adjectives were used instead of prepositional phrases—"Franklin Elementary PTA" instead of "PTA *of the* Franklin Elementary School." I also avoided unnecessary words in using simple verb forms like "to plan" and "will meet" instead of "will *hold* a meeting."

As your stories grow longer than the illustrative notice in Example 4, they will lose their punch in a morass of roundabout phrases, boring passivity and unnecessary words. Furthermore, the reader will be less inclined to read a long story which does not catch his interest in the first paragraph.

In addition, as stories become longer, they will contain more facts. The jumble will become even more perplexing if you do not use the Five W's to organize your information.

Instead of dashing headlong into a story, I strongly recommend that you categorize your facts under the various "W's" on paper until you become proficient enough to recognize important elements on sight and to organize the material in your head.

Once your facts are stacked into piles of "W's"—like boards and barrels of nails—you will be ready to build your story, remembering, though, that unlike buildings, news stories start with the roof—the apex of the news triangle—which is the lead.

MORE COMPLEX STORIES

The "notice" in Example 4 is the simplest type of release you will have to write. Use Example 4 as a model in such cases, substituting the appropriate "W's" for your organization.

These notices usually do not get a separate headline. They often are grouped with similar announcements under what are called "standing headlines," like "MEET-

INGS," "CLUB ANNOUNCEMENTS," "TOWN NOTES" or "COMMUNITY BULLETIN BOARD."

"Standing heads" are typographical expedients and help to control repetition in headlines such as "PTA to Meet," "VFW to Meet," "Boy Scouts to Meet," and so on.

More complex stories, of course, will require more than one paragraph and probably will contain more than one who, what, when, where and why. It will be helpful, then, to examine the Five W's more closely to see that their usual respective functions are in most news stories.

As in the case of the simple announcement, the elements of the lead most often will be "who" or "what" or a combination of both.

Verbs are always "what" elements because they tell the reader *what* the subject is doing or *what* is being done to the subject. It may be helpful for you to think of the "who" element as the subject of your lead and the "what" as the following verb.

The "when" and "where" elements are usually not the most significant aspects of the news story. They can be used in the body or they can be used to tie the lead paragraph together. "When" and "where" leads might be used in a *feature* story, and these will be discussed in the next chapter.

The "why" element is generally developmental, although it, too, might provide a feature story lead. Sometimes, however, an apparent "why" element actually will be a "what" in disguise and, as such, may deserve a place in the lead.

We will consider the possibility of converting "why" elements to "what's" in the following example, illustrating a story about an organization event.

ORGANIZATION EVENTS

Organizations may be formed for a variety of reasons. Poetry clubs meet solely for intellectual discussions about verse; taxpayer groups act as watchdogs on the local government; and PTA's provide equipment and programs to maintain quality education within the community.

Whatever their reasons for being, these organizations from time to time sponsor various projects—a local poet is asked to give a reading, or the PTA raises money to buy encyclopedias for the school library.

We will use the PTA to illustrate the preparation and development of stories about organization events.

In Example 4, we isolated the following W's:

Who—The Franklin Elementary PTA.

What—will meet.

When—on Tuesday night at 8.

Where—in the school cafeteria.

Why—to plan a rummage sale.

Let us suppose that the rummage sale proceeds will be used to buy encyclopedias for the school library. We must list this new piece of information under one of the five W's.

As neither a person nor an organization, the idea of buying encyclopedias for the school library cannot be grouped under "who." It is neither a place nor a time, so "where" and "when" are out.

On the other hand, the buying of encyclopedias is the reason for the rummage sale, just as the rummage sale is the reason for the meeting. We shall place this new information in the "why" category, where we now have:

Why—to plan a rummage sale and to buy encyclopedias for the school library.

If we were to leave this new information in the "why" category, however, we would be overlooking a strong lead element. As I pointed out, "what" elements sometimes masquerade as "why's."

In Example 4, the meeting was our "what" and the planning of the rummage sale was "why" the meeting was called. But the rummage sale itself might be considered an event, just like the meeting, and be placed in the "what" category. Instead of saying "will meet" in our lead, we might have said "will hold a rummage sale" or "will plan a rummage sale."

Our new lead could read like this:

The Franklin Elementary PTA will hold a rummage sale on Saturday from 9 to 4 in the school gymnasium.

Similarly, we can move the idea of buying encyclopedias into the "what" category.

What does that accomplish? By progressing from a commonplace event (the meeting) through a more specific event (the rummage sale), we arrive at the idea of buying encyclopedias for the school library. That is the ultimate goal of the PTA and has more *news value* than either the meeting or the rummage sale.

The idea of buying encyclopedias for the school library is what makes this story different. A meeting is a meeting, no matter what organization conducts it. Likewise, many organizations hold fund-raising events and it makes little difference if the event is a rummage sale or a car wash or anything else. It is the *purpose* of the event and not the event itself which makes a story more unusual.

The ultimate purpose of the meeting and the rummage sale is to buy encyclopedias for the school library. That ultimate purpose will be the story's lead. By assembling your facts under the Five W's and then analyzing those facts for the most newsworthy element, the task of choosing a lead element becomes a relatively simple process.

The non-professional, then, is well advised to examine the "why" category to make sure he is not overlooking a strong lead element.

In the following example, notice that we have several "what" elements and have introduced a new "why" to replace the two elements we re-categorized under "what."

Example 5
   The Franklin Elementary PTA (*who*) **will buy encyclopedias for the school library** (*what*).
   At a meeting (*what*) **on Tuesday night at 8** (*when*) **in the school cafeteria** (*where*), **the PTA will plan a rummage sale** (*what*) **to raise funds for the project** (*why*).

Example 5 has a strong lead. It will earn a separate headline, something like the following:

PTA WILL BUY
LIBRARY BOOKS

SHOTGUN LEADS

As stories grow more complex, there is a tendency among non-professionals to try to cram many facts into the lead. The effect is like the blast of a shotgun as compared to the precise aim of a rifle.

In addition to buying encyclopedias for the school library, for example, the PTA also may have established standing committees, filled vacant offices, appointed an *ad hoc* committee to plan a holiday party, and any number of other things.

In stories which contain many elements in the "what" category, you must take careful aim to choose the most important item, as was done in Example 5.

Once the lead element is recognized, you can summarize all additional business in the second paragraph and begin to develop the lead in the third paragraph; or you may finish with the lead element before turning to "other business" in some subsequent paragraph in the body.

In either case, introduce the "other business" by means of a transitional phrase like: "In other business, the PTA. . . ."

SERIES STORIES

Whatever event your club is sponsoring, you want to publicize it to improve its chances of success.

Keeping in mind newspaper policies on multiple submissions, which were discussed in Chapter 4, you plan a series of articles. In that series, each story must have a different lead—some fresh slant—which is achieved by selecting different lead elements from the list of "W's."

The most newsworthy element in Example 5 is the idea of buying encyclopedias for the school library. Example 5 would make a good "kickoff" article for your series.

The following examples illustrate the use of different elements to provide fresh leads:

—Example 6 reports the formation of a committee to plan the rummage sale mentioned in Example 5.

—Example 7 leads with the rummage sale itself and probably should be filed the week before the sale is to be held.

Example 6
The Franklin Elementary PTA last night appointed a rummage sale committee.

The committee, under Chairman John Thomas, will organize a sale to raise money to buy new encyclopedias for the school library.

Also serving on the committee will be Mary Wilson and Margaret Johnson.

Chairman Thomas said the committee will hold its first meeting on Tuesday night at 8 at his home, 123 Riverside Drive.

Example 6 used a lead taken from the "what" category. See if you can pick out other elements and list them under the appropriate Five W headings.

In Example 6, the release date would be the day

following the committee appointment. Note that the time reference "last night" was used in the lead.

If a release follows an event by several days, some papers use a time reference such as "recently," rather than a specific date which might make the piece seem stale. Remember that news value diminishes with time and always try to file a story as soon after an event occurs as possible.

Example 7 uses still another approach to the rummage sale story—the sale itself. It also keeps the purpose of the sale—buying encyclopedias—in the reader's mind (the sale is for a worthwhile project).

Example 7
The Franklin Elementary PTA will hold a rummage sale on Saturday from 9 to 5 in the school gymnasium.

The sale, which is being held to raise money for new encyclopedias for the school library, will feature booths for clothing, furniture and bric-a-brac.

John Thomas, sale chairman, said anyone who would like to contribute sale items may contact him.

In addition to using a fresh lead, Example 7 provides new information. It tells the reader what items will be sold and also lets people know that usable items gathering dust in their attics or basements may be donated to a worthy cause.

After the sale is over, the PTA president may want to thank the public for its support. In writing this story, do not begin with the statement of thanks; furthermore, when you do express the president's gratitude, quote him directly, putting the "thank you" in his voice rather than the paper's.

Your release could read like the one in Example 8.

Example 8
The Franklin Elementary School yesterday received a new set of encyclopedias, donated by the local PTA.

> **In a brief ceremony at the school library, James Whitmore, chief librarian, praised the PTA as "an important organization which provides a valuable service to the local school district."**
>
> **PTA President Jane Doe said the project would not have succeeded without the support of the public.**
>
> **"I want to thank all the citizens of Anytown who supported our recent rummage sale, either by purchasing items or by donating merchandise for sale," she said.**

In stories like Example 8, exercise caution and restraint in phrasing the compliments between the library and the PTA so that your piece does not sound like a gushing back-slapping contest.

On the other hand, keep your ears open for remarks like Whitmore's. You do not want to get carried away, but moderate praise from an official makes your organization look good.

Another point to keep in mind about series articles is not to flood the local paper with releases. If you do, you will wear out interest in your subject, much like politicians who begin their campaigns too soon. After your kickoff piece, plan several shorter articles, to be followed by another strong-lead story just before the event you are writing about occurs.

Returning to Example 8, in addition to the principles of grammar which were covered in Chapter 5, notice the variety of paragraph beginnings.

The first and third paragraphs begin with proper nouns used as the subject of the sentence.

The second paragraph begins with a prepositional phrase.

The fourth paragraph is introduced by a direct quotation.

In addition to grammar and variety in paragraph beginnings, news style (Chapter 3) also will give your stories a more professional sound.

AN "EAR" FOR NEWS

Many of you may have heard it said about a reporter that he has "a nose for news." A good reporter will "smell out" a story that his colleagues of lesser talent might overlook.

You, too, will have to develop "a nose for news" by becoming able to recognize news value so that you can elevate your stories above the routine.

But the beginning news writer must also develop an "ear for news." In Chapter 5, for example, I talked about the use of grammar to produce a professional news sound.

Given enough exposure to stories written by professional journalists, a writer, in time, probably would learn to "parrot" the sound of news. Studying professionally written stories by knowing what to look for, then, will help to develop your news ear.

If your local newspaper subscribes to any of the major news services—United Press International and the Associated Press—you can be certain that those stories have been written by professionals.

News service stories are identified in the *dateline,* which is found at the beginning of the article and includes the place of origin of the story and the news service designation. The news service designation is abbreviated and placed inside parentheses. The following dateline, for example, indicates an Associated Press story which originated in Chicago:

CHICAGO (AP)—Mayor Richard Daley said last night. . . .

I suggest that you identify news service stories in your local paper and study them for the following:

    —The use of the Five W's and the selection of the lead element from one of those categories.

—The different ways in which paragraphs are
   begun.
—Consistent use of style.
—Rules of grammar covered in Chapter 5.

NEGATIVE LEADS

Just as your lead should answer rather than ask a
question, it should also broach the story from a *positive*
rather than a negative point of view. You do not normally
begin a story by saying that something did *not* happen.

But suppose the PTA rummage sale which we used
in previous examples did *not* succeed in raising enough
money to buy encyclopedias. The situation is a negative
one. How can a negative story be approached from a
positive point of view?

The question just posed is not a difficult one to
answer; in fact, there are three answers:

—Examine the Five W's to find the reason why whatever was supposed to happen did not happen and
   begin your story with a "why" lead.
—If what was expected to happen did not, but something else happened in its place, begin with what
   did happen.
—If neither of the first two solutions is appropriate,
   your lead should use a *verb* which *expresses* negativity rather than the negative *adverb* "not."

To illustrate the first solution to the negative lead
problem, let us suppose that it rained on the day of the
rummage sale and that temperatures turned unusually
cold. If the "what" of this story is that the rummage sale
did not succeed, then the "why" category would include
"rain" and "cold" as the reasons. Rather than write "The
Franklin Elementary PTA did not raise enough money to
buy new encyclopedias for the school library," you could
begin with a "why" lead similar to the one in Example 9:

Example 9
Rainy, cold weather was blamed for the failure of the Franklin Elementary PTA to raise enough money to buy new encyclopedias for the school library.
Few braved the elements to attend a PTA rummage sale which was held on the school grounds.

The previous is a good example of a "why" lead.

Professional reporters may be guilty of negative leads. I know one reporter who frequently writes: "No one was injured in a collision last night on Route 1." The following headline actually has been used for such a lead:

NO ONE HURT
IN COLLISION

To illustrate the second solution to the negative lead problem, the lead just given can be written to stress what *did* happen: "Two cars collided on Route 1 last night. No one was injured."

This alternative to the negative lead applies just as well to the failure of the PTA rummage sale.

Suppose the PTA raises only $100, which is about one-third of what it needs to buy the encyclopedias. If the weather were bad, $100 might be more than one would have expected under the circumstances.

In writing a lead which stresses the positive you can come up with Example 10:

Example 10
The PTA raised $100 at a rummage sale yesterday, in spite of bad weather which kept attendance down.
"It's only about one-third of what we need to buy encyclopedias for the school library," PTA President Jane Doe said, "but I think the results were very good, under the circumstances."

If there is no apparent reason for the failure of an event, or if you can find nothing positive to write about, your lead at least should be constructed with a verb which *expresses* negativity rather than with the negative adverb "not."

Example 11
    Negative adverb: The Franklin Elementary PTA did *not* raise enough money to buy encyclopedias for the school library.
    Negative verb: The Franklin Elementary PTA *failed* to raise enough money to buy encyclopedias for the school library.

The negative verb is preferred to the adverb "not" because the verb expresses something that happened: The PTA *failed.* That statement is more positive in tone, if not in meaning, than one which uses "not." If you write "The PTA did *not* succeed," the tone is entirely negative.

IMPROVING THE LEAD

Points to keep in mind about writing a strong lead are summarized below:
    —Select your lead element from the Five W's, but do not *force* each of the Five W's into the first paragraph.
    —The lead should be direct (active voice), declarative (do not ask questions), and positive (use a "why" lead; find something positive; or, use a negative verb rather than the adverb "not").
    —Try to limit your lead to no more than five lines; preferably, three or four lines.
    —Use incidental information to "flesh out" the body of your story or in transition from one paragraph to another.
    —Do not back into a story by leading with irrelevant information such as the time and place of a meeting already held. Get to the point at once.
    —Avoid using too many statistics in the lead. Statis-

tics are difficult to digest and, even in the body of the story, should be used selectively. If you are uncertain about what statistics are important or what certain statistics mean, consult the source or some local "expert" whom you can quote.

—Learn to boil down complicated statements. Again, consult an expert if you need help. Do not be afraid to paraphrase as long as you have verified that your interpretation of a complicated statement is accurate.

—Avoid generalized leads which sound impressive but which actually say nothing substantive. Say something specific; tell the reader something he may not have known before. The generalized lead will be dealt with later in this chapter under the section which deals with guest speakers.

—Report your facts in logical sequence, beginning with the most important. Do not allow important facts to float unnoticed in the body of the story.

In Examples 12 and 14, I use actual news releases from non-professional publicity chairmen to illustrate faulty leads. After criticizing those examples to show where the writer went wrong, I illustrate improved versions of those leads in Examples 13 and 15.

Example 12
Faulty lead: The Anytown Women's Club announced that its regular monthly meeting for October will be held on Tuesday night at the Anytown American Legion at 7:30 p.m. with Mrs. John Doe, president, presiding.

Mr. Jack Jones, vice president of the Anytown Montessori Association, will be guest speaker. He will present a program on Montessori education.

There are so many things wrong with Example 12 that it is difficult to decide where to begin. By now, you should be able to recognize many of the faults.

The most serious fault is that the writer chose the

wrong lead element. The most newsworthy element contained in Example 12 is the appearance by a guest speaker; that should have been the lead.

I will use the guest speaker lead in Example 13, but a stronger lead might develop if you can find out what Jones is going to say. Example 21 illustrates such a lead.

If you cannot find out what Jones is going to say, you can eliminate the last sentence in Example 12 altogether. To say that a Montessori educator is going to speak about Montessori education is ridiculously obvious.

But missing the lead element was not the only mistake made by the writer of Example 12.

The use of "regular," "monthly," and "October" to refer to the meeting is redundant. If a meeting is held "monthly," that *is* "regular." You might refer to the "October" meeting and let it go at that. Actually, the only reference you need to make to the meeting is when and where it will be held.

Nor was logical sequence followed in the first paragraph of Example 12. The day and time of the meeting should have been written together because they are related facts.

Moreover, you will notice that the writer used both "night" and "P.M." which is redundant. As I explained in Chapter 3, "night" is preferable to "P.M." but the choice will depend in all cases upon local style. In no case, however, should you use both "night" and "P.M."

"Mrs. John Doe, president, presiding" is not only redundant, it is an example of crowding the lead with incidental information.

If Mrs. Doe had something important to say, her statement might be worth using as the lead. Otherwise, the reference to her as president is better used as a transition element to begin the second paragraph or some other paragraph in the body.

In Example 12, the writer also backed into the story

by using the "announced that" construction, followed by a passive voice verb "will be held." The lead would be stronger and more to the point if the writer had eliminated "announced that" and used an active construction.

Another consideration of style involves the use of "Mr." with "Jack Jones." If the local paper uses polite forms of address, "Mr." is acceptable; if polite titles are not used, "Mr." should have been omitted. If "Jack Jones" has a Ph.D. degree, however, the writer could have referred to him as "Dr. Jack Jones."

With these objections in mind, let us consider a different approach to the information in Example 12, beginning, this time, by categorizing the facts under the Five W's.

Here are the facts from Example 12:

—Who: The Anytown Women's Club; Mrs. John
  Doe, club president; Jack Jones, vice president of
  the Montessori Association.
—What: A club meeting; the appearance of a guest
  speaker; a program about Montessori education.
—When: Tuesday night at 7:30.
—Where: The Anytown American Legion.
—Why: The reason for the meeting is to hear Jack
  Jones, the guest speaker.

Jack Jones is appearing to tell the club members about the Montessori method of education. The program about the Montessori method is being held because there is interest among the club members in its techniques.

The "who" and "what" categories most often produce the lead element of any story. Lacking an important statement from the club president and an important club project, Jack Jones seems to offer the best choice for a lead with his program about Montessori education.

Remember, however, to examine the "why" category for possible lead elements which may have been overlooked. As I said, if the "why" category included specific points which Jones expected to cover, those points might have been used in the lead.

Nevertheless, using only the facts provided in Example 12, notice how the faults have been eliminated in Example 13.

Example 13
    Improved Lead: Dr. Jack Jones, a local authority on Montessori education, will address the Anytown Women's Club on Tuesday night at 7:30 in the American Legion home.

A more appropriate lead element has been chosen for Example 13. The time elements are grouped. The active voice "will address" is used. Redundancies and incidental information are eliminated.

Example 13 is an *improved* lead but it still is not a *strong* one. Its main weakness is that is is too general, too vague, to be of interest to anyone outside your club.

Broadening your stories so that they will appeal to the public and not just members of your club ought to be one of your goals as publicity chairman.

If you had available a specific statement from Jones' talk as your lead in Example 13, for example, you would have made it stronger. If you were unable to contact Jones, you could have used a brief statement about Montessori education itself: What is it? How does it differ from conventional education?

We will return to the discussion of widening the appeal of your stories shortly. First, let us consider another example of a faulty lead. Example 14 contains many of the same faults we found in Example 12.

Example 14
    Faulty lead: The Mothers Guild of SS. Peter and Paul Church held a monthly meeting recently and 11 new members were accepted into the club.

Here again the writer backed into the story. The lead element is the admission of 11 people into the organization. That information should have begun the story.

Time references like "recently" usually are omitted because they imply that a story is old stuff.

"Monthly" is unimportant information which only gets in the way of the story.

Here is how Example 14 might have been written:

Example 15
   Improved lead: Eleven people were inducted by the SS. Peter and Paul Mothers Guild in a ceremony held at the church.

Notice the use of the passive voice "were inducted" in Example 15. As I said in Chapter 5, the passive voice is a legitimate construction. I used it in this case because I wanted to get the lead element as close to the beginning of the story as possible.

Using the active voice, the sentence would have read: "SS. Peter and Paul Mothers Guild inducted 11 people in a ceremony held at the church."

The active voice is preferred, but if the passive will get the reader to the point of the story faster and without complicating the sentence, by all means use it.

REPORTS ABOUT MEETINGS

In addition to writing advance stories about projects which your organization is planning, you frequently will write reports about what went on at meetings already held.

Even a routine meeting contains some news value. The degree of news value depends upon how many people will be interested in the particular information you wish to impart.

Some meetings are of interest only to the members,

others may discuss items of importance to the public-at-large. We will consider first an example of a meeting of interest to members alone.

Let us suppose that the PTA elected officers at its meeting. Your lead might be as follows:

Example 16
The Franklin Elementary PTA last night elected officers for 1974–75.

More often than not, the non-professional will overlook the lead element and submit stories which begin like the following:

Example 17
The Franklin Elementary PTA held a meeting last night in the school cafeteria. An election of officers was held, with the following elected to serve terms for 1974–75.

By now, you should be able to identify the faults in stories like Example 17. The lead element was missed and the story is redundant and too wordy.

The degree of news value also depends upon your ability to identify unusual elements which will elevate the story above the routine.

Suppose one of those elected by the PTA was Jane Doe, who will be serving her third consecutive term as president. That information is not of earth-shattering significance, but it does make for a stronger lead.

Example 18
Jane Doe was elected to her third consecutive term as president of the Franklin Elementary PTA.
At a meeting last night, the PTA also elected John Thomas, vice president; Jane Ardmore, treasurer, and Thomas Jenkins, secretary.

In Example 18, I again used the passive voice to move the lead element to the beginning of the story. For practice, try writing Example 18 in the active voice.

WIDENING APPEAL

Learning to recognize unusual elements is part of developing your nose for news. Often, the result will be a story which appeals to people outside your organization. The rewards will be more public interest in what your club is doing, which will mean, perhaps, a larger, more active membership. In addition, wider appeal means more news value and better play for your stories.

Widening appeal was mentioned among suggestions for improving Example 12. Another example which comes to mind involves absenteeism.

Many non-professionals allude indirectly to the problem of absenteeism with a favorite concluding sentence: "All members are urged to attend."

A former colleague would eliminate that sentence with one enthusiastic stroke of his editing pencil. Not only does it violate the newspaper's voice, but, more important, the news value lurking just below the surface of that sentence is being ignored: If absenteeism is a problem, it is worth writing about, especially if it is likely to have an indirect effect on the community.

The following example deals with the problem of absenteeism as more than a concern to PTA members alone. Much news value, as it turns out, is contained in this seemingly routine problem.

Example 19

Absenteeism is threatening to dissolve the Franklin Elementary PTA, according to President Jane Doe.

"We had hoped to buy encyclopedias for the school library," Doe said, "but we had to abandon a fund-raising project because not enough members turned out to help with the arrangements."

"If attendance continues to decline, we will give up and go home," Doe said.

If the PTA does "give up and go home," the schools would lose a source of financial aid, she said.

Last year, the PTA raised more than $1,000 to buy

new microscopes for the science department. The year before, it bought wall maps for the history classes.

"If it were not for the PTA," Doe said, "those items would have to be bought with tax dollars or not bought at all."

"It isn't just a PTA problem," she said, "taxes affect all of us."

Example 19 deals with a situation of considerable importance, but crisis is not the only criterion for wide appeal.

Many local organizations provide wheelchairs, walkers and other medical aids to members of the community; others are concerned with recreation for youth and adults alike; some offer cultural programs; and still others operate a community ambulance or provide volunteer fire protection.

I have used the PTA in most of these examples to avoid confusion in illustrating various stages of development in the news story. I could just as easily have substituted the Lions Club, the VFW, church societies, library groups, hospital auxiliaries and other civic, social and service organizations typically found in communities all across the country.

It does not matter if your story is to be about a PTA rummage sale or making finger sponges for the local hospital, the news writing procedure is the same.

THE GUEST SPEAKER

The final type of story I will cover in this chapter is the report on appearances by guest speakers, whose topics may be of interest to the public as well as to organization members.

The news writing principles you have learned so far still apply, of course, but there are some special considerations which must be given to guest speaker stories:

—You must identify the point of the talk, the "what" element. Be specific.

—You must include data which support the speaker's position (but not *too* many statistics). These data are the "why" or "how" elements.

—You must establish the authority of the speaker. This is the "who" element.

The first of these three guides is the old problem of recognizing the lead element of the story. You must decide what the speaker is advocating or opposing. The speech itself is actually a verbal essay and the lead element should be the speaker's topic sentence.

It is helpful to get an advance copy of the speech. Doing so enables you to familiarize yourself with the speaker's remarks before the speech is delivered, thereby improving your understanding of it. A printed copy of the speech also helps you to review the text, which is difficult during the course of its actual delivery. If you have a written copy, you may circle unclear portions of the speech and question the speaker about them afterward for clarification.

If the speaker talks extemporaneously or from an outline rather than from a prepared text, you have to take notes. Jot down statements which you find interesting and questions which occur to you to be asked during the post-speech interview.

I used to take copious notes when I began in this business, but experience has led me to have more confidence in my powers of recall and to avoid taking detailed notes during the course of a speech. It's a good idea to jot down specific figures for the sake of accuracy, but trying to copy verbatim statements from verbal delivery can be distracting, even if you use shorthand. You will be surprised at how much you will remember by listening attentively while the speech is being delivered. You can get direct quotes and verify statistical data in an interview later with the speaker. Still, you may feel more secure in taking longer notes at first. Go right ahead.

The second guide evolves from what we already have learned about story development. We follow the lead element with arguments which the speaker used to support his main statement. These data are used to construct the body of the news triangle.

However, take care in writing the body of this or any other type of story not to glut the article with statistics. In large doses, statististics force the reader to analyze material for what is significant; that, really, is your job.

Analyzing statistics and boiling down complex statements which the speaker may use are all part of becoming a good news writer. Above all, however, you must be accurate.

Any journalist worthy of the title will do his best to make sure he has all the facts. If his information and interpretations are constantly open to challenge, he loses credibility. Without credibility, he cannot function as a reporter.

In analyzing statistics and statements of guest speakers, then, you must be sure that your interpretation is consistent with the speaker's intent.

The last of the three guides represents the greatest departure from our previous considerations of the Five W's.

The "who" element takes on new and greater importance in the guest speaker story because the speaker must have some expertise for his remarks to carry weight. Without expertise, the speaker's conclusions and opinions concerning his topic may be no more valid than yours or mine or any other layman's.

To establish the significance of the speaker's remarks, therefore, establish his authority as soon as possible; if not in the lead itself, then in the second paragraph.

Establishing the authority of the speaker, however, does not mean that you must present his life history. A common shortcoming of most non-professionals is to begin with the speaker's date of birth and continue with virtually every experience he has encountered in his lifetime.

The speaker's occupation or profession is generally sufficient to establish his authority, or, if he is a public official, his title will do.

Like statistics, too much biographical data slows up the story. If a person's biography is interesting enough, the story possibly could be written as a feature instead of as a news article.

With these three guides in mind, here is an example I prepared from an actual news release. It illustrates how *not* to write a guest speaker story.

Example 20
    State Auditor General John Doe of Middlebury was a guest speaker at the dinner meeting of the Johnstown Rotary Club. Introduced by Sam Jones, the speaker discussed his work, presenting many interesting comments about state activities.

He spoke of some of the state laws involving his department and discussed his department's relationship with other state agencies. He noted that the handling of public money deserves stringent controls.

The story was longer than this, but I am stopping it here to consider where it went wrong.

The most glaring weakness is that the story deals with generalities and matters which really could be taken for granted: "the speaker discussed his work"; presented "many interesting comments about state activities"; "spoke of some state laws involving his department"; "discussed his department's relationship with other state agencies."

The story's lead is what we referred to earlier in this

chapter as a "say nothing" lead. Not only that, the lead is cluttered with unimportant information without regard for logical sequence.

As written, Example 20 tells the reader nothing of importance.

The only statement which shows any promise at all is: "He noted that the handling of public money deserves stringent control."

That last statement is merely "noted" and yet it is the only concrete statement the speaker has made—at least, it is the only concrete statement the writer has given the speaker credit for.

The reader has had to endure two paragraphs of incidental information. The writer gives the auditor general's home town, whatever bearing that has; mentions the dinner meeting of the club; and throws in Sam Jones, whoever he is, just for good measure. *That* is a cluttered lead!

Only in identifying the speaker as auditor general has the writer come close to following our three guides.

Let us suppose that the need for stringent controls on public spending is the speaker's topic sentence and proceed with an example which follows the three guides I suggested.

In the following example, I have had to imagine the "many interesting comments" which the writer alluded to in Example 20.

Example 21
   State Auditor General John Doe called for "more stringent controls on government spending" in an address last night to the Johnstown Rotary Club.
   Doe blamed rising taxes, in part, on "duplication of effort within state government."
   Citing a two-year study by the State Economy League, Doe said an "overstaffed bureaucracy" wastes $2.5-million of the taxpayers' money annually because of "overlapping duties among state agencies."

He said that waste could be eliminated if his office were used as a "clearing house" for state expenditures.

Example 21 recognized the "many interesting comments" mentioned in Example 20 and shares them with the reader. Example 21 is more interesting than Example 20, in part, because it has been more *specific*. Some readers may agree that controls are needed and others may disagree, but at least the reader has something specific to ponder. We would hope, too, that Doe has said something the reader did not know before reading the story and that his comments will give the reader fresh insight into state government operations.

The story is also more interesting because we have eliminated irrelevant information contained in Example 20. After specifically stating the point of Doe's talk, the story *proceeds logically* to explain why Doe feels controls are needed and cites a study which supports Doe's contention.

Following our three guides, Example 21 also sets the authority of the speaker by identifying him as a public official who is in a position to know what is going on within state government.

Of course, the organization which sponsored the talk will want—indeed it deserves—credit for arranging the program. Note how unobtrusively the Johnstown Rotary Club was inserted in the lead. It follows the topic sentence incidentally, rather than competing with it as it did in Example 20.

In dealing with "expert" speakers, don't be intimidated by the authority the speaker commands. Do not be afraid to question him about things you do not understand in order to get specific information for your story. Do not be afraid of asking a "silly" question; if the speaker is sincerely interested in his topic, he will want you and the rest of the public to know exactly what he is talking about.

WHAT THE FUSS IS ABOUT

The goal of this book is to produce more professional articles and to turn humdrum, routine stories into more interesting news pieces.

Following the advice I offer will do much to improve your skills as a news writer and your reputation in the eyes of the editors with whom you will be dealing.

No matter how important your own organization's activities may seem to you, stories about those activities compete with hundreds of other, similar stories for valuable news space and, once in print, for the reader's attention.

Before the reader ever sees your story, it will be read by an editor. Well-written stories which look and sound professional are more likely to get bigger headlines and better position in the news pages. Stories which get good play are more likely to attract the reader's attention.

The basic rules of news writing do not vary greatly for the feature story, which we are about to examine.

For the feature, too, if you use a professional format, follow local news style, apply the rules of grammar and learn how to construct a solid, tight story, your articles will be more effective. Both you and your local editors will be the beneficiaries.

7

The Feature Story

YOUR CHANCE TO BE CREATIVE

The requirement for objectivity, which was discussed in Chapter 5, and the method of constructing a news story according to a "formula" which produces the news triangle, covered in Chapter 6, admittedly limit the writer's freedom of expression.

But, if the confining structure of the news story is a hindrance to the writer's creativity, it also gives the beginning news writer a solid framework upon which to hang his facts and a tested blueprint which directs him step by step from the point of assembling those facts to the conclusion of the article. The publicity chairman who has never prepared a news release before, in a quandary over how to begin, has the security of a proven formula which will give him the results he desires.

The feature story, however, is not as easy to mold into a standard formula.

In the news story, the writer is concerned only with a set of facts which will convey information to the reader. The requirement for objectivity limits subjective comment by the writer, whose only task is to present his facts as quickly and as clearly as possible. The use of a formula makes that task easier and gives the news story its crisp tone.

Of course, the feature contains facts too. Those facts are assembled under the Five W's just as they were for the news story. The difference is that the facts in a feature story are handled more subjectively than the facts of a news story. The information must be as accurate as it was for the news story and the writer must not slant a feature in such a way that it gives the reader an impression which is not true, but the writer does have a great deal more leeway in style (in the literary sense) when writing a feature than he does within the news story structure.

The feature recognizes *unusual* relationships among the facts of a story and relates those facts in such a way as to evoke an emotional response from the reader. The news story may evoke certain emotions, too, but if that occurs it must be a result of the facts by themselves and not a result of some prepossession of the writer. The appearance of emotions in the feature story is what causes it to be more subjective than the news story.

Setting out to evoke an emotional response from the reader requires the exercise of imagination. Your success in feature writing will depend on your ability to use your imagination to recognize unusual elements within the body of facts you have assembled. Many reporters who produce crisp news stories could not write a feature if their lives depended upon it.

Already, then, we encounter two differences between news stories and features: (1) the feature resists formulization; (2) the feature is more subjective and seeks to evoke an emotional response.

In other words, the feature is your chance to be creative, but the nature of creativity is such that it is difficult to provide anything but a general guide. It is one thing to give a person a numbered drawing and tell him to apply paint No. 1 to space No. 1 and quite another to expect him to produce a finished painting with all its lines and tones on a blank canvas solely from his imagination.

Most of the stories you will write will be news stories, which are like paint-by-number drawings. If, however, you are able to develop the ability to recognize unusual elements within a given body of facts, you may be able to produce an occasional original painting, which is the feature story. A feature twist gives an otherwise routine article an individuality which sets it apart from many other, similar stories which are competing for the same news space.

In this chapter, we discuss modifications to the basic news triangle, human interest as an important feature story ingredient, extraordinary elements of time and place, and the use of the pun, dramatic irony and dramatic imagery to evoke emotional responses.

MODIFYING THE NEWS TRIANGLE

The news triangle is the fundamental blueprint for straight news stories. Using the most important fact in the lead paragraph and following with less important facts in the body produces a news triangle like the one in Figure 1.

Figure 1

```
              X                          lead
             XXX
            XXXXX
           XXXXXXX                       body
          XXXXXXXXX
         XXXXXXXXXXX
```

For the sake of illustration, let us consider a story about Jane Doe, who will receive the PTA's "Member of the Year" Award. Written as a straight news story in the structure of Figure 1, such an article would go something like this:

Example 1   **(lead)**
   Jane Doe will receive the Franklin Elementary PTA "Member of the Year" Award in a ceremony tomorrow night at the school.
                         (body)
   In making the announcement, PTA President John Smith said, "Although this award specifies a period of one year, the recipient's total contribution to the PTA since becoming a member must be considered."
   "In the 10 years she has been a member, Jane Doe has demonstrated a willingness to participate in the activities of the PTA, which often required the sacrifice of her own free time," Smith said.

Example 1 represents a story which most club publicity chairmen are called upon to write. It follows the basic news triangle in Figure 1, combining a "who" and a "what" for the lead paragraph, followed by information which comprises the body of the story.

However, in Chapter 6 you were advised to try to make your stories appeal to as many readers as possible. Example 1 is not a bad lead. It follows the news triangle presented in Chapter 6, but it is likely to appeal only to members of the Franklin PTA and to people who know Jane Doe. This is where the feature comes in.

Many organizations present awards of one kind or another. If you use your imagination to find an element which elevates Example 1 above the general category of "awards stories," you may be able to attract more readers.

In Example 2, we will rewrite the straight news account of Jane Doe's award, this time using a feature approach.

Let us suppose that the PTA holds its meetings on Wednesday nights, and, furthermore, that Jane Doe has a husband for whom she must prepare a meal every night. Perhaps Jane Doe serves him TV dinners on Wednesday nights to give herself time to attend the PTA meetings.

The main point of Example 2 still is Jane Doe's award, but to elevate this story above the routine, a writer with a healthy imagination will give the piece a feature twist. Giving a story feature treatment, however, often means that the basic news triangle has to be modified. The lead will be delayed for a paragraph or two until you "hook" the reader with some element which will catch his interest.

In the case of Example 2, the lead element, which is Jane Doe's award, is delayed until the third paragraph in order to "hook" the reader with an anecdote about TV dinners.

Example 2
For the last 10 years, Wednesday supper at Jane Doe's house has consisted of TV dinners.

The reason is that the Franklin Elementary PTA meets on Wednesday nights and, in the last decade, Jane Doe has attended all but a handful of those meetings.

The reward for her involvement in PTA activities will come tomorrow night when she receives the PTA's "Member of the Year" award.

As is the case with most news stories and features, the lead combines a "who" and a "what." Emphasizing the human interest angle in Example 2 with the anecdote about the TV dinners delays the lead to achieve the feature twist.

The result is a new story structure which actually consists of *two* triangles. Instead of a lead *paragraph*, we have a lead *triangle* which is turned upside down. The lead *paragraph* of the lead *triangle* occurs as usual at the apex, only this time the triangle is inverted. At the same time, the lead paragraph forms the apex of a second triangle in normal position and supplementary facts expand to form the body of the story.

It may be helpful to think of the lead triangle as an "introduction" to the story. At any rate, the first modification to the basic news triangle is illustrated in Figure 2.

Figure 2

```
                XXXXXXX
                 XXXXX              lead triangle
                  XXX
                   X                lead paragraph
                  XXX
                 XXXXX
                XXXXXXX             body triangle
               XXXXXXXXX
              XXXXXXXXXXX
```

In Example 2, the lead was delayed until the third paragraph. As shown in Figure 2, the lead is in the fourth paragraph; or, it could have been placed in the second. It is also possible to delay the lead until the final paragraph, but such stories are rare and mentioned more for your information than as a suggestion for actual use. Stories such as those illustrated by Figure 3 build to a dramatic conclusion. In fiction, O. Henry was famous for these "trick ending" stories, but they are not as simple as they appear.

Figure 3

```
              XXXXXXXXXXX
               XXXXXXXXX
                XXXXXXX            body
                 XXXXX
                  XXX
                   X               lead
```

The non-professional should keep in mind, however, that modifications to the basic news triangle in Figure 1 require experience. Features themselves and modifications to the basic news triangle, which will usually resemble Figure 2, should not be attempted until you have become thoroughly familiar with the preliminary material covered in Chapter 1 through Chapter 5 and the news story form presented in Chapter 6. The feature will be your final level of sophistication within the journalistic genre.

Even when you graduate to features, you should stick to the basic news triangle initially. To illustrate a story with a feature twist which follows the basic triangle, let us rewrite Example 2.

Example 3
   When Jane Doe receives the Franklin Elementary PTA's "Member of the Year" award tomorrow night, she probably will say a silent prayer for TV dinners.
   In the last decade, Mrs. Doe has missed only a handful of PTA meetings. Serving TV dinners to her husband on Wednesday nights has been part of the reason why.
   Wednesday night is the regular meeting time of the PTA and Mrs. Doe said, "I could never make the meetings if I had to prepare and cook a meal."

The stories in Examples 2 and 3 are not beyond the experience of most club publicity chairmen, but some imagination and a bit of extra effort are required.

The hard facts of Jane Doe's award story are readily available. The anecdotal material is harder to come by.

As you gain experience, begin to look for unusual elements in any story that you are called upon to write. Features occur less frequently than news stories, but they should not be overlooked.

If you are assigned to write about Jane Doe's award, call her on the telephone or drop by her home for an

informal chat. You may come up with an amusing anecdote like the one about TV dinners.

The leads in Examples 2 and 3 make the reader ask:
"What in the world do TV dinners have to do with this
woman's receiving an award?" He is hooked. Even those
who neither know Jane Doe nor belong to the PTA will be
inclined to read the story.

LEAD TABOOS

Before examining other elements of the feature
story, keep in mind that negative leads and interrogative
leads are nearly as objectionable in features as they were
in news articles.

As in the news story, your goal in the feature is to
answer questions, not ask them. Likewise, your approach
should be positive rather than negative.

You may, of course, plant a question in the reader's
mind, as already explained, but avoid asking him a question directly. Negative and interrogative leads are as in-
dicative of amateurism in the feature as they were in the
news story.

HUMAN INTEREST

As was pointed out earlier in this chapter, the feature will evoke an emotional response from the reader.

Emphasizing the "who" of the story through human
interest anecdotes is an effective way of evoking an emotional response.

The feature lead, like that of the straight news story,
often is a combination of "who" and "what." That was the
case in Examples 2 and 3. When human interest is in-
jected into the story, however, "who" takes on more importance than it did in the news article. For example, the
"who" element might overshadow the "what" if the per-

son we happen to be writing about is someone of the stature of the President of the United States.

If you or I should stub his toe on an airplane ramp, hardly anyone is likely to notice. When President Ford did exactly that, the story made page one.

But a person need not be a celebrity to command the reader's interest.

Let us consider an example in which a local organization runs a program which helps ex-convicts find legitimate jobs when they get out of jail.

The program is the "what" of the story, but if we choose the feature approach instead of the straight news angle, we inject an element of human interest which increases the importance of the "who" element.

Example 4
   Some men are doctors, lawyers, or even Indian chiefs, but for nearly three-quarters of his life, John Doe has been a thief.

This example will be used shortly to illustrate the use of dramatic imagery and is expanded at the end of this chapter to further illustrate the format which was recommended in Chapter 2.

The story which appears at the end of this chapter uses the news triangle modification which was illustrated in Figure 2. Example 5, which follows, also is a variation of Figure 2. The point of the story is to publicize a program which helps ex-convicts to find jobs; that lead element is delayed only until the second paragraph, long enough to hook the reader with a feature twist.

Example 5
   Some men are doctors, lawyers, or even Indian chiefs, but for nearly three-quarters of his life, John Doe has been a thief.
   Whether or not he remains a thief will depend upon the success or failure of a local experimental program to find jobs for convicts after they leave prison.

Hooked by the human interest angle, the reader will go on to learn about a worthwhile program. Mission accomplished.

In using the human interest approach, I am also illustrating an example of a "who" element lead. We will consider examples of leads taken from the rest of the Five W's, but first there are some other characteristics of the feature to consider.

Human interest is an important ingredient in feature writing, but it is by no means the only device we use to hook the reader.

Is there anything in Examples 4 and 5 besides human interest which makes you want to read this story about a thief named John Doe? Does the story show imagination? Does it evoke some emotional response? Does it promise to relate an experience which you have never had or one which you may never have? These questions lead to a better understanding of what the feature is and how it differs from the straight news article.

We already have discussed imagination and emotional response, but let us take a look at the promise of an experience we may not have had.

VICARIOUS EXPERIENCE

Another frequent ingredient in a feature story is the opportunity for a reader to experience something he is not likely to experience on his own—an African safari, perhaps, or a prison sentence.

Most of the children who skipped rope to the chant alluded to in Examples 4 and 5 probably grew up to enter "respectable" vocations. As adults, they may tell occasional lies or misappropriate a few ballpoint pens from the office, but they are not what society would classify as hardened criminals.

Instead of dealing with a rehabilitation program, as in Example 5, this feature could be written about John Doe's life in prison. The reader will experience jail to some degree through John Doe.

DRAMATIC IMAGERY

Examples 4 and 5 allude to a childhood rope-skipping chant that conjures an image designed to increase the dramatic impact upon the reader. As I recall, the chant went something like this:

Rich man, poor man, beggar man, thief,
Doctor, lawyer, Indian chief.

Images used dramatically catch the reader's interest. No one can create your images for you. They must come from your own creative instincts. They may derive from childhood experiences, such as the one above, or, perhaps, from literature. The image may parallel the real-life situation and show similarity, or it may contrast with real life.

In Examples 4 and 5, the image of innocent childhood, conjured by the rhyme, is juxtaposed with the image of a man who grew up to be a thief. Symbolic innocence is juxtaposed with literal guilt. Such juxtapositions may evoke sadness or joy or pity or any other emotion.

SELECTING THE PROPER IMAGE

In using images to evoke an emotional response, take care not to let your imagination run away with you. The image you choose must be logical; there must be some connection between the image and the subject of the story.

Furthermore, the image should not be so arcane that the reader cannot visualize it. If the reader cannot relate to the image you choose, the image is worthless.

On the other hand, do not use an image that is trite or corny. One emotional response you do not want to evoke from the reader is a groan.

Finally, exercising your imagination must not become an end in itself. Do not use the feature solely to show the reader how clever you are or to parade your knowledge pedantically in front of him.

In the feature, as in the news story, remember, simplicity remains the best rule.

GILDING THE LILY

Take care not to abuse the freedom which the feature offers.

In feature writing, as in anything else, avoid excesses. Learn to avoid writing syrupy pieces which gush with sentimentality, at one extreme, and one-sided diatribes which bristle with blatant hostility at the other.

Objectivity cannot be disregarded altogether. It must be used to check exaggeration and to give the feature true proportions in which the importance and relevance of the subject are not distorted.

If, as you read over your finished feature, bands begin to play and fireworks explode in the back of your mind, or if plaintive strains of violins issue from your subconscious, you probably are guilty of "gilding the lily." Try writing the piece again with more restraint. The reader should be able to *sense* the sound of the violin without actually hearing it.

In features which are overwritten, the writer's bias is too obvious and the reader is likely to be skeptical of what he is being told. If that happens, the effect of the piece will be lost.

USING THE PUN

Puns may be used to give a story a feature twist. It is in the use of the pun that the non-professional must exercise caution against being corny. Another failing in the use of the pun is that the link between the pun itself and the subject of the story is so tenuous that the reader must stretch his own imagination to the breaking point to rationalize the play on words.

In this section, a "what" lead will be used to illustrate how a pun might set up a feature.

I use a story which recently crossed my desk. Written as a straight news piece, the story was about a peanut sale to raise money for a local club project. Once again, imagination is important in turning a routine *news* release into a more interesting *feature*.

In Example 6, I use the Franklin Elementary PTA once again to show how the piece was written by the club publicity chairman and then I rewrite the story in Example 7, giving it a feature twist.

Example 6
The Franklin Elementary PTA met on Friday night for its regular monthly meeting. President John Doe presided.

President Doe suggested that the organization hold a peanut sale in order to raise money to buy a new set of encyclopedias for the school library.

After a unanimous vote, the PTA agreed to begin the sale on Monday, June 1, with PTA members conducting a door-to-door canvass to take orders.

By now, it should be obvious to you how that story should have been written. The peanut sale, which was the lead element, was buried in the body of the story. In addition, the original release was single spaced and typed in capital letters. It left no space for instructions to the printers and it contained many simple mistakes in grammar and spelling.

If at least some of the rules already presented in this book had been followed, I might have had time to re-write the lead paragraph, giving it a feature twist by playing on the word "peanut."

If I had had the time, I could have rewritten the lead like this:

Example 7
The Franklin Elementary PTA will be working for "peanuts," but members hope to earn more than that in a fund drive which will begin on June 1.

On that date, the PTA members will begin selling peanuts door-to-door throughout Anytown. They will be trying to raise enough money to buy new encyclopedias for the school library.

By playing on the word "peanut," a routine fund drive story takes a feature twist which elevates it above the ordinary. It is this kind of opportunity that should not be overlooked.

A headline written for Example 6 might say:

**PTA WILL HOLD
FUND CAMPAIGN**

If I had had time to re-write the lead, as I did in Example 7, or, even better, if the writer had thought of it himself, the story could have carried a more eye-catching headline:

**PTA TO RAISE FUNDS
WORKING FOR PEANUTS**

LOOK FOR THE UNUSUAL

As in the previous example, it is often necessary to use your imagination to look beyond the obvious facts of a story to uncover elements which lend themselves to feature treatment.

Example 8 shows what can be done with another routine story by using your imagination to look deeper into the facts assembled under the Five W's.

The lead element comes from the "what" category. The story will announce the opening of a church bazaar.

Example 8, like Examples 6 and 7, comes from an actual case involving a former colleague, now retired after 35 years as a journalist.

Church bazaars are popular in the area where I live. Equally popular are the potato pancakes which are served in enormous quantities at these neighborhood social affairs. My colleague, who was features editor at a local newspaper, helped his church publicize its bazaar, much to the church's benefit.

In the hands of a beginner, the story probably would have begun: "The St. Nicholas Church bazaar will be held in the church parking lot on Main Street from July 5 to July 7."

But instead of the typical "church to hold bazaar" story, my friend computed how many pancakes had been made at the bazaar a year earlier, then, based upon the average size of a potato pancake, he figured that if all those pancakes were laid end to end they would reach from the door of the church to the door of the newspaper where he hoped to have the story published. I might add that the church and the newspaper were about two blocks apart on the same street.

If that were not enough, he found out how many potato pancakes would be made for the current bazaar and decided that the church would produce enough pancakes to reach beyond the newspaper to a high school one more block away.

Example 8
     If all the potato pancakes sold at the St. Nicholas Church bazaar last year were laid end to end, they would have reached from the church to the front door of this

newspaper. This year, the church will try to reach Any-town High School.

The headline for this story said:

**CHURCH POTATO PANCAKE MAKERS
OUT TO TOP SPUD-TACULAR FEAT**

It should be apparent to you now why the feature is so hard to define in a standard formula. The boundaries of the feature are defined primarily by the limits of your imagination.

UNUSUAL TIME OR PLACE

Unusual elements in the "when" and "where" categories are ready-made for feature treatment. Of the two, the "when" is likely to occur more frequently.

An example of an unusual "where" element for a feature lead might be if the local astronomy club is going to meet in an open field situated at an elevated spot to observe a lunar eclipse. Such a story might also include an unusual time for the meeting. Those elements can be taken advantage of to take the story out of the ordinary "club to meet" category.

The same person who produced the potato pancake story also came up with the piece used in Example 9.

A member of the local Moose lodge, he wrote a short piece announcing an election of lodge officers. It just so happened that the lodge election fell on Nov. 7, the same day as the local municipal election.

Instead of an unimaginative "Moose lodge to elect officers" story, he produced a much more interesting lead:

Example 9
Members of Moose Lodge 123 will vote twice today, but it will all be legal.

As is the case with all the examples used in this book, Example 9 could just as easily have been about the PTA elections or the elections of any other club. It remains for the club publicity chairman to recognize the opportunity for feature treatment.

Nor does a feature story have to run on for a dozen paragraphs or more. The desire for simplicity remains in the feature as it did in the news story. The freedom offered by the feature does not license the writer to pad a story with verbose phrasings and irrelevant facts.

When completed, Example 9 consisted of one additional paragraph which contained the specifics of the Moose election, giving the time and place and explaining "why" it would be legal for the members to vote twice on General Election Day (once for municipal officers and once for club officers).

Three of the Five W's were contained in the first paragraph:

Who—members of Moose Lodge 123.

What—will vote (hooking the reader with the double vote and delaying the lead "what" element, which was the Moose lodge election, until the second paragraph. The story had the configuration illustrated in Figure 3).

When—today (the release date of the article coincided with the date of the elections).

This professional writer used his imagination to give a feature twist to a routine club event, making it far more interesting than it would have been if it had been written as a straight news story.

Even though the entire piece consisted of just two paragraphs, the imaginative feature lead was enough to earn it special treatment on one of the more prominent news pages. Dozens of similar stories carried in the same edition and written as routine "club to elect officers" pieces were buried on pages where they received far less notice.

As far as the "where" category is concerned, a club member's visit to a foreign country or any other unusual place might be handled as a feature instead of as a straight news release.

Club members often address their organizations after returning from trips, and invariably, these stories begin as dryly as: "So and so will present a program at the next meeting of such and such a club." These stories could be improved greatly with a little extra effort on the part of the club publicity chairman.

Suppose, for example, that a PTA member from Iowa has just returned from a convention held by that organization in Philadelphia. Many non-professionals begin such a story as follows:

Example 10
     The Anytown PTA will meet on Tuesday night at 8 in the school cafeteria, at which time John Doe will report on the PTA convention held in Philadelphia.

The writer has attended to the Five W's but the piece is flat. Certainly, the delegates to the convention discussed many items of interest. Perhaps one of the items discussed was the need to create greater interest in PTA activities among the members of the community. A story like Example 10 will do little to achieve that goal.

On the other hand, if John Doe can report on something of interest to the local community, he may succeed in attracting new members.

Suppose that John Doe learned about a program in which students were invited to become members of the PTA. That information is worth reporting to the local community back home in Iowa.

Example 11
     A group of Philadelphians has added another letter to the PTA. That letter is "S" and it stands for "students."
     Recognizing the importance of soliciting students' views on education in order to plan new school programs and revamp old ones, the Parent-Teacher Associa-

tions in Philadelphia have invited students to become active PTA members.

Results from these new PTSA's are encouraging, according to local PTA delegate John Doe.

Doe will report on this new idea at a meeting of the Anytown PTA on Tuesday night at 8 in the school cafeteria. In keeping with the spirit of his talk, students as well as other non-members of the PTA have been invited to attend.

The story could go on to present a few "teases" about some of the questions residents and local PTA members might have about such a program.

For example, Doe might comment briefly about how seriously the students take their new responsibility or how the program helps to interest the young people of a town in community affairs by listening to their views instead of ignoring them.

As a club publicity chairman, you have to remain alert for opportunities which will interest the rest of the community in what your organization is trying to accomplish.

DRAMATIC IRONY

Another useful device for hooking the reader with a feature twist is the use of *dramatic irony,* in which a given cause leads to an unexpected effect.

To illustrate this device, let us return to the rehabilitation program for ex-convicts which was used in Examples 4 and 5.

This time, let us suppose that former thief John Doe is the man in charge of a rehabilitation program. The use of irony may be an effective way of getting into this story.

Example 12
One man's failures may lead to success for convicts being released from County Prison.

John Doe, a former thief, is in charge of a local

program designed to find legitimate jobs for ex-convicts in Jones County.

Cooperating with Doe in the project are local business and professional people who are concerned about what they see as "the failure of the present penal system to rehabilitate criminals."

"I was going nowhere," Doe said recently. "I must have been in and out of reform schools and prisons at least a dozen times by the time I was 25."

"The last time I got out I swore I'd never go back. I was lucky enough to find a man who had faith in me and who gave me the training I needed to earn an honest living," he said.

That man is William Smith, a local electrician, who taught Doe his trade, but the fact that Doe is "someone who's been there," as he puts it, has helped to make the local program a success.

"The cons trust me," Doe said, "because I know what it's all about. They know their sob stories won't work on me and they respect me because I've been where they've been. People who have never been behind bars just can't understand why some people become criminals."

Example 12 uses dramatic irony to illustrate a feature lead taken from the "why" category. Because John Doe has failed and because he does not want to fail again, he may be able to help others achieve the success he has achieved.

Compared with Examples 4 and 5, Example 12 also illustrates that there is more than one way to approach a story. Once again, the importance of being able to use your imagination emerges.

ENDING THE FEATURE

So far, I have been discussing how to begin a feature. Unlike the news story, however, how a feature ends is almost as important as how it begins.

If you can figure out a way to end a story which ties the whole thing up in a neat package, your feature will be improved. A possible ending for Jane Doe's award is illustrated in Example 13. If you find it difficult to come up with a catchy ending for a feature, however, remember simply that any story ends when it is over.

For the sake of illustration, then, I will resurrect Example 2. We begin as we did before.

Example 13
For the last 10 years, Wednesday supper at Jane Doe's house has consisted of TV dinners.
The reason is that the Franklin Elementary PTA meets on Wednesday nights and in the last decade Jane Doe has attended all but a handful of those meetings.
The reward for her involvement in PTA activities will come tomorrow night when she receives the PTA's "Member of the Year" award.

At this point, you would continue with the specifics of the award, comments from the PTA president, or whatever else you wished to say, working up to your final paragraph.

Perhaps in talking with Jane Doe, you learned that she and her husband have a running joke about the Wednesday TV dinners. Mrs. Doe might quip that perhaps her husband's name should be on the plaque with hers.

Mrs. Doe's quip can provide just the ending you are looking for. Consider the following as a possible ending for Example 13:

In commenting on the award, Mrs. Doe said that the subject of TV dinners on Wednesday nights has become an inside joke between her and her husband.
"In fact," she said, "maybe the PTA should put his name on the plaque with mine. After all, he's the one who has had to eat all those TV dinners."

FEATURE OPPORTUNITIES

Publicity writers for organizations which operate on a full-time basis and which deal with programs involving

ex-convicts, for example, probably will have more opportunities to write features than the average club publicity
chairman.

Even when you do produce a human interest feature
from the local PTA, you may find that the *degree* of
human interest may not be as great as in, say, the story
about the ex-thief.

Still, the feature is an effective way of elevating ordinary "announcement" stories or other routine pieces
above the commonplace. Features take more effort and
imagination, but the result in terms of increased reader
interest in what your club is doing will be worth it.

While it is difficult to give a standard formula to
follow in writing a feature, the suggestions included in
this chapter should at least help you to understand the
difference between a news story and a feature and get
you started in the right direction.

The following example is somewhat different from
the feature which I began earlier. I offer it to illustrate
the format presented in Chapter 2, using some of the
rules of style and grammar presented earlier to further
illustrate how a complete feature might sound.

Jobs for ex-cons

Exclusive to The Daily News

Release before Thursday, Oct. 1

W. C. Line
123 Any Street
Your Town
987-2345

     Two weeks ago, John Doe celebrated his 22nd
birthday in Cell Block "A" in the county prison.
At an age when many young men are getting out of
college, Doe was looking forward to getting out of
jail. Doe will be released from prison next Thursday.
Whether or not he returns, as many like him do, remains
to be seen.

        --more--

first add--jobs for ex-cons

Largely, it will depend upon him, but it also will
depend upon whether or not anyone is willing to show him
alternatives to a life of crime--alternatives he had not
noticed by himself.

Doe may be luckier than most young men in his
position. Silver City does give alternatives to ex-
convicts through a program called "Jobs After Jail."

Administered by the state's Department of Corrections, the program is sponsored by a group of local
businessmen who are willing to give ex-convicts a
second chance.

George Roberts is one of those businessmen. He
owns a printing shop.

"Look, there are some people who want to be
criminals," Roberts said. "But there are also ex-
convicts who really want to go straight, only they'll
never make it without help."

--more--

130

second add--jobs for ex-cons

    "Those of us in this program feel that offering jobs
to ex-convicts who want to stay out of jail is one way of
helping," Roberts said. "After that, it's up to the
individual."

    When Doe leaves prison on Thursday, his new apprentice-
ship will begin at once. He will report directly to Roberts,
who will show him around the shop and introduce him to the
other employees.

    "Being accepted by his fellow workers will be
important for Doe," Roberts said. "Exposure to non-
criminals will help him learn a new set of values."

    On Friday and Saturday, Doe will observe how the
printing operation is run, getting the "feel" of his new
surroundings.

    Thomas Williams, who is warden at the county prison,
described the first three days of the program as "an
orientation period."

--more--

third add--jobs for ex-cons

"Observing for a few days helps a man ease into the
program," Williams said. "We don't want to frustrate a man
by expecting him right off the bat to do a job he hasn't
been trained to do."

"We don't believe in 'the shock treatment,'"
Williams said, "but it is important to keep him from
immediately getting back in touch with his old comrades."

"If we release a man on Thursday and leave him
on his own over the weekend," Williams said, "chances are
that he'll be back here on Monday instead of at his new
job. More often than not, men who are released in the
morning with nowhere to go will have stolen a car or
robbed a liquor store before the day is over."

Williams is optimistic about the program.

--more--

"We're just getting started," he said, "but in the six or seven months since the program began, we've already noticed a marked decline in the rate of recidivism."

Recidivism describes the tendency for criminals to remain criminals.

"Prisons have really been schools for criminals," Williams said. "We're trying to change that. We're trying to give these men some alternatives."

On Thursday, one school will be over for John Doe and another will begin. He will have his alternatives. The rest will be up to him.

--30--

133

8

Photographs

SOMETHING EXTRA

From time to time, you will have the opportunity to use pictures with the news and feature stories you write.

Newspapers have preferences for certain kinds of photos and aversions towards others. After checking with your local editor, include those preferences in a special section on photographs in your stylebook.

Some of the things you have to consider in using photos are: size and quality, static versus action shots, some of the costs involved when photos are used, how to group several persons for the best effect, and how to write "cutlines" to accompany photos.

A picture is worth a thousand words. That old aphorism is true; but pictures which do not complement the stories which they accompany or photos of poor quality and those which are poorly composed are virtually worthless.

One of the goals of this book is to help you elevate your news release above the routine and pictures must work to that end as well as the text of the story.

It should be pointed out, too, that photos have a subsidiary function as far as newspapers are concerned. Pages which consist only of type are said to be "gray." Editors use photos to break up that gray matter and make the news pages more interesting.

It is the aim of this chapter to help you produce effective photographs to accompany your releases. We address that task now.

SIZE

The standard, recommended photo for newspaper use is an 8″ × 10″, black and white, glossy print.

Newspapers and other periodicals can use pictures which are larger or smaller than the standard 8 × 10, but you can't go wrong with this recommended size. Check with the editor for the size of photos desired.

PICTURE QUALITY

The reproduction of a picture in a newspaper can be of no better quality than the original print. For that reason, seriously consider the use of a professional photographer, preferably one who has had experience in newspaper photography. His equipment and expertise will surpass whatever is available to you from within your club, unless, of course, you happen to have a commercial photographer or a talented amateur within your midst.

Cost, however, may be a governing factor and we will deal with that shortly.

If your club cannot afford to hire a professional, you will be relieved to know that your local newspaper probably will accept pictures which are less than ideal.

One of the most frequent questions I am asked by club publicity chairmen is whether or not Polaroid pictures are suitable for newspaper use.

Polaroids and other cameras manufactured for non-professional or "family" use may be used to take news photos, but keep in mind that more expensive, professional-use cameras with more finely ground lenses will produce better results.

Likewise, color prints may be used but they generally yield quality which is inferior to black and white photos when reproduced in black and white on the newspaper page.

Check with your local paper to see what restrictions it imposes.

PICTURE COSTS

Commercial studios and freelancers are in the *business* of taking pictures. They charge fees. Price will vary from place to place but, to give you some idea of the costs involved, one freelancer whom I know charges $7 for one print if the photo is taken during usual working hours and up to $9 for night and holiday jobs.

In the same city, a commercial studio which my paper uses will charge from $10 to $12 and up for similar service.

In addition to the photographer's charges, your local paper may charge for the extra handling required to make negatives or engravings for use of pictures with stories.

The cost to the newspaper for reproducing a photograph depends on the type of printing process used. Papers produced by letterpress, the familiar lead type, require photoengravings called "cuts" or "half tones." However, many newspapers now are printed by offset methods and usually no cuts are needed in this process.

The photograph is stripped into a page with "cold type" and rephotographed.

"Cuts" may range in price from $5 or $6 to $10 or $12 or more, depending upon the size of the finished engraving.

Between photographer fees and engraving charges, then, you can expect to incur costs in the neighborhood of $15 to $20 if you plan to use a single photo with a story.

One club publicity chairman recently called to complain about engraving charges. He had used two pictures with his release and the engraving charge was $23. That did not include the photographer's fee.

If your local paper imposes charges for the use of photos, remember to include a billing address on the back of the photo.

Check with the paper you intend to use. If an editor feels your story has sufficient news value, he may assign a staff photographer, if the paper has one, to take your pictures without charge.

Likewise, some papers impose no charges for picture reproduction; or, if they do, those charges may be suspended if a story has sufficient news value or if the paper has a policy which suspends charges for certain categories of pictures, such as servicemen or non-profit organizations.

GROUP PHOTOS

All pictures draw attention because they break up the gray columns of type. Still, try to avoid using pictures in which people are arranged in rows. These pictures all look alike, and, except for a momentary glance, will attract little interest from the reader.

It is much better to use photos in which the subjects are doing something. We will consider action pictures later in this chapter, but the use of static, group photos seems to be a cross which most small-town editors must bear.

If you must use static, group pictures, at least learn how to arrange your subjects to get the best effect.

One of the most common failings of group pictures is that the subjects are strung out in a line from right to left. That kind of grouping is illustrated in Figure 1.

Figure 1

O O O O O O O O O O O O O O O O O O

Pictures in which the subjects are arranged as they are in Figure 1 will include unimportant background and foreground details which will be "cropped" out—eliminated—from the picture as it appears in the newspaper. When a picture like Figure 1 is cropped, the end result will be a photo which is out of proportion. Cropping from the top and bottom will produce a picture which is too wide for its depth (the vertical or "top to bottom" measurement of a picture).

It helps if you limit the number of subjects in a photo to as few as possible. If you do, cropping will be less of a problem; the camera can get closer, making the subjects larger and the overall result will be improved.

Still, I can sympathize with the publicity chairman whose fellow club members all want to appear in a photo. There are 18 subjects in Figure 1 and I recommend that you stay within that limit. If you include any more than 18 people, the subjects will be difficult to recognize in the paper, unless the editor allows for an unusually large photo, which he is not likely to do for pictures of this type. Again, check with the editor as to the maximum number of persons he permits in a photograph.

I will offer some suggestions on how to arrange various numbers of subjects up to 18. Following these suggestions will give you pictures of desirable proportions and the subjects will be recognizable when the photo is reproduced in the newspaper.

The proportions we are after are those in which the width of the longest row (the rows should be fairly equal) is roughly twice the depth, measured from the top of the head of the tallest person in the back row to the waist of the shortest person in the front row.

In the case of any photo in which there are two rows or more, the tallest people should be positioned in the back row, with the tallest of *those* in the center and progressively shorter people toward each end of the row in a kind of slanted-roof effect. The tallest person, then, should be in the center of the back row and the shortest person should be at either end of the front row.

In arranging group photos, it is helpful to use a staircase or have some persons seated, if no other means of elevation is available.

Now let us consider some of the arrangements possible for groups of up to 18 people. The only thing to keep in mind in the following diagrams is that the subjects in the back rows will have to be placed slightly to the left or right of the people in front of them so their faces are not blocked.

I recommend that you put no more than six people in any single row when arranging groups of up to 18 people. If you have seven, for example, split the group into two rows, with three in the first row and four in the second. Suggested arrangements are illustrated in Figure 2.

As I said, try to have no more than 18 people in any one group. If you do, just remember to arrange your subjects so that the width-to-depth proportion of the picture is roughly two to one.

Before moving on to other arrangements, it is important that you note one important exception to grouping for height among the subjects. If prominent people

Figure 2

up to six people
0 0 0 0 0 0

seven people
0 0 0 0
 0 0 0

eight people
0 0 0 0
 0 0 0 0

nine people
0 0 0 0 0
 0 0 0 0

ten people
0 0 0 0 0
 0 0 0 0 0

eleven people
0 0 0 0 0 0
 0 0 0 0 0

twelve people
0 0 0 0 0 0
 0 0 0 0 0 0

thirteen people
0 0 0 0 0
 0 0 0 0
 0 0 0 0

fourteen people
0 0 0 0 0
0 0 0 0 0
 0 0 0 0

fifteen people
0 0 0 0 0 0
 0 0 0 0 0
 0 0 0 0

sixteen people
0 0 0 0 0 0
 0 0 0 0 0
 0 0 0 0 0

seventeen people
0 0 0 0 0 0
0 0 0 0 0 0
 0 0 0 0 0

eighteen people
0 0 0 0 0 0
0 0 0 0 0 0
0 0 0 0 0 0

appear in the picture—your club officers or the town mayor, for example—try to center these people in the front row. If height presents a problem, have them seated, again, trying to place the tallest in the center.

VERTICAL COMPOSITION

The arrangements suggested above will produce pictures which are wider than they are deep. That *horizontal composition* is recommended for large groups.

For pictures in which there will be fewer than six people, *vertical composition* may be more effective.

Vertical composition always is used for "portrait" pictures of single persons, for example. If there will be two people in a picture, the subjects should be positioned close enough together to achieve a vertical effect.

Other groupings which lend themselves to vertical composition are:

— Three persons, two of whom are standing behind one seated.

— Four persons, two of whom are standing behind two seated.

— Five persons, three of whom are standing behind two seated.

Having some of the subjects seated increases the vertical effect. Each of the above groupings is illustrated in Figure 3.

Figure 3

```
    0 0                                      0 0
     0                                       0 0
               0 0 0
                0 0
```

As in horizontal composition, a two to one ratio is suggested for vertical pictures, except, of course, the depth in vertical photos should be about twice the width.

SOMETHING DIFFERENT

If your local paper uses static group shots, the arrangements suggested in Figure 2 and Figure 3 will produce pictures of desirable proportions, which will be an improvement over the photos most non-professionals submit with their releases. Still, group photos are not especially interesting and you should try to come up with a picture that will help to elevate your release above the routine. What is required is the same use of imagination which is needed to produce a good news or feature lead.

In trying to come up with alternatives to standard group shots, many non-professionals will pose a subject at a desk and holding a pen or sheet of paper in his hand. You also undoubtedly have seen pictures in which two people are shaking hands or in which one subject is passing a certificate or a check or a trophy to another subject.

While such attempts to come up with something different are commendable, pictures such as those I have just described are only slightly better than static group shots. The subjects *look* posed and there still is little action.

A good example of "posed" pictures is provided by a club in the area where I live. Each month, this club chooses an outstanding student from the local school district. The "Outstanding Student" program is a good one, but each month the club submits a photo which shows the club president handing a certificate to the winner of the award. Neither the picture nor the story represents anything out of the ordinary.

If the club publicity chairman were more imaginative, he could produce a short feature about each month's "Outstanding Student."

Perhaps one month's winner is interested in archaeology and plans to pursue that interest in college. The student may be able to supply a picture of himself working in some archaeological digs as part of a summer program. If not, he may have a collection of artifacts with which he can be posed for a picture to accompany the story. The feature, of course, would be broached with this interest in archaeology.

Another "Outstanding Student" might be planning a career in aeronautical engineering and have an impressive collection of model airplanes upon which the picture and story could be based.

Given an interesting feature and picture each

month, an editor can arrange to have the "Outstanding Student" Award run as a regular series. A monthly feature like that would do much to draw interest and support for the club involved.

To consider another example, suppose that you, as club publicity chairman, are to write a piece about an essay contest which your club is sponsoring. If the contest is successful, you may receive hundreds of entries.

Many organizations wait until such contests are over and then submit photos in which the winner is receiving his certificate and the congratulations of the president of the organization, while the runners-up and other officers look on.

With a bit of imagination, you can write a news release to run while the contest is still in progress. Place the contest judge at a table with the "mountain" of entries piled in front of him. You might have him cradle his head in one hand with a look of comic exasperation on his face.

Being alert for situations such as the one just given not only will produce pictures which are out of the ordinary, but also present an opportunity to publicize an event with a release about a portion of that event which otherwise would have been overlooked. Such situations are especially important if you have planned a series of stories about a single event.

Another example is a club which will offer handmade afghans as prizes in a fund-raising drive. Use a picture which shows the women actually at work on the afghans.

The suggestions for pictures used with the "Outstanding Student" Award, the PTA essay contest and the handmade afghans all are preferable to static shots of people assembled in rows.

What I am suggesting is that you exercise your imagination and use it as you would in writing a feature.

You may be able to come up with a picture idea which is out of the ordinary, one which will make the reader take notice.

As in the feature, no one can teach you to be creative; one can only hope to show you where the path to more imaginative photos begins.

WRITING CUTLINES

Whether you are able to produce interesting action photos or whether you must settle for a group photo, you still have to describe what the picture is about. That description is given in a short blurb called a "cutline."

Sometimes, the entire text of a story will be carried as cutlines under a photo. That style usually is used only when the text consists of no more than two or three paragraphs. Cutlines usually are brief.

For longer stories, some significant point of the text is extracted, condensed and used in the cutlines with the names of the subjects who appear in the picture.

Newspapers have different styles which govern how identifications in cutlines are to be made. The following are some points of style to look for in your local paper. Cutline style should be included in your stylebook:

—Usual cutline style calls for identification of subjects from left to right.

—If you wish to begin the identification with someone who is not at the extreme left of the photo, you may do so as long as local style is followed. In such cases, does your local paper prefer commas—John Doe, center,—or parentheses—John Doe (center)?

—When giving the names of the subjects in a photo, does the paper allow the use of one initial with the last name—J. Doe—or does it prefer the full first name—John Doe? Most papers which require full names will allow *two* initials and the last name: J. W. Doe.

—In groups arranged in rows, does the local paper prefer to begin with the front row and move to the rear, or does it begin with the back row and move to the front?

—Does the paper use "from left to right" or, simply, "from the left"?

—Does the paper use "front row," "middle row," "back row"; or does it prefer "first row," "second row," "third row" or "row one," "row two," "row three" or "row 1," "row 2," "row 3"? Does local style allow "standing" and "seated" when appropriate?

—Does the paper drop the phrase "from left to right" after the first row or is the phrase retained throughout?

—Does the paper begin a new paragraph for each row, or does it include all rows in a single paragraph, separating the rows by semicolons?

The best advice, given the wide range of styles which exists, is to examine your local paper thoroughly to find out the style it uses in cutlines in a majority of cases. You may find that style is modified for special types of pictures. Paste these style samples in your stylebook and remember to refer to them whenever you use photographs with stories.

Cutlines always should be written on a separate sheet of paper and, like the text, should be typed in capital and lower case letters and be double spaced. Do not write on the backs of photographs as the pen or pencil's impression may mar the face of the picture.

In the upper left-hand corner of the cutline sheet, write the story slug, followed by the word "cutlines": "handmade afghans—cutlines."

When including pictures with news releases, submit the photo, text and cutlines at the same time. That practice is insurance against the components being separated and lost.

When you have completed the cutlines, do not attach them to the picture. Assemble the text, the cutlines, and the photo and clip them together with a paper clip. Do not use staples.

Here is one tip in securing the names of the subjects in a group picture. I carry a few extra pens or pencils and some 3×5 index cards. I simply start one card at the left of each row and ask each subject to *print* his full name and pass the card on to the next subject in line until the card reaches the end of the row. I collect the completed cards at the end of each row and my identifications are made with very little trouble. Of course, the cards are numbered to correspond to each row before the cards are distributed. And subjects are asked to print their names to avoid confusion as to spelling.

Another thing to remember is that when submitting more than one picture, the cutlines for each should be individualized so if two photos are used the cutlines will not repeat each other.

POLICY TABOOS

Examine your local paper thoroughly to see what kinds of pictures it uses. Most will use group shots and all like good action pictures.

Still, there may be certain subjects which are taboo, either because they are in poor taste or because they are so routine that the paper would be deluged by many similar photos.

For example, the paper for which I work will not use a picture in which alcoholic beverages are displayed.

Therefore, have subjects put down glasses before facing the camera.

As an example of pictures which are too routine, we no longer use photographs of four generations within a single family. Such photos are so commonplace that other families would want equal space and the paper could not hope to accommodate all the requests.

In dealing with these taboos, exercise judgment. If, for example, a paper does not use pictures of children enrolled in tap-dancing lessons, it still may consider newsworthy a picture of a juvenile performer who won a regional competition.

If you can develop an eye for photos in the same way that you develop an ear and a nose for news, your organization will be the beneficiary of better news coverage.

The next chapter is included to give you some idea of how a newspaper operates and to help you better understand the reasons behind much of what is covered in this book.

9

Newspaper Organization

A GENERAL VIEW

The means by which newspapers process news from source to printed page will vary greatly. A paper like the *New York Times,* for example, will have a complex structure which includes an international staff of editorial and administrative personnel. On the other hand, some very small papers may be operated by a handful of people and have a circulation area which may extend no further than the town or county boundaries. More than likely, it is a newspaper similar to the latter with which you will be dealing.

Generally speaking, the newspaper operation may be broken up into five areas of responsibility:

—Administrative. This department includes the publisher, who may also be the owner of the paper, and a staff of secretaries, bookkeepers and other personnel whose job it is to see that the

149

newspaper functions as a business and who have no direct role in the gathering and presentation of the news itself.

—Advertising. This is the department which pays the bills, so to speak. The revenue from advertising pays the salaries of the people employed at the newspaper and the expenses involved in producing the newspaper itself—newsprint, ink, machines, maintenance and so forth.

—Newsroom. The collection of editors, reporters, and photographers which make up the editorial staff of the paper is the department which is directly involved with the gathering and processing of news.

—Mechanical. The mechanical departments actually "construct" the finished newspaper. The process begins in the composing room, where reporters' stories are set in type, and ends in the press room, where the finished newspaper rolls from the printing press.

—Circulation. Once the newspapers roll off the presses, it is the job of the circulation department to deliver the papers to points of distribution to be purchased by the public.

This, admittedly, is a greatly simplified view of how a newspaper operates. It is provided merely to illustrate that the editorial department—the one with which you will be dealing—is not an independent operation but one which must be coordinated with many others.

WHERE DO YOU COME IN?

When you submit an article to your local paper, you become, in effect, an extension of your newspaper's staff. That role may be more important than you realize, especially if your local newspaper is a small one.

This book probably will be as beneficial to your local editor in terms of eliminating "busy work" as it is to you in improving the effectiveness of your news releases. The less editing required to get your articles into print, the more valuable you become as an extension of the local newspaper staff.

Styles and policies often are established to help the news department mesh more smoothly with the other departments involved in newspaper production.

If you follow the suggestions for typing, format, grammar, construction of news and feature stories, and pictures, you will help the local editor to process articles more quickly. No newspaper, whether a daily or a weekly, can afford to have news stories backing up in the editorial department. In many cases, editors discard releases because they simply do not have the time to spend on ill-prepared copy.

Your local paper probably has a staff large enough only to cover what the editor determines to be major news events. It cannot hope to assign a staff reporter to every meeting of the PTA, Lions Club, church group and other organizations.

Without club publicity chairmen like you, many worthwhile programs might fail because the public simply was not aware of their existence and the community would lose the benefits of those programs.

But your potential value as an extension of the local news staff is severely diminished if an editor must spend time on busy work like simple spelling and grammatical errors.

Likewise, stories which must be rewritten are little help to busy newspaper editors. The same is true of copy which is submitted in longhand and must be typed by a member of the staff before it can be processed.

Nor is an editor likely to look kindly upon copy which forces him to squeeze corrections into single-

spaced lines or which does not leave him room to give
directions to the composing room.

If an editor is confronted by a story which requires
too much of his time, he may decide that the work required to maintain whatever standards he has set is simply not warranted by the news value of the article in
question. In such cases, the release will wind up in the
wastepaper basket.

There is too much competition for news space for
you to assume that an editor will automatically correct
your errors in every case.

EDITING COPY

Not only does an editor deal with scores of news
stories each day, but he has other duties as well, all of
which place demands upon his time.

When an editor receives a news story, he must check
it for errors in style, grammar, spelling and word usage,
as indicated in previous chapters. The less errors in those
categories the better. But the correction of simple errors
is by no means the only task of good editing.

For one thing, an editor must also be on the alert for
inconsistencies. A news release announces a meeting of
the PTA on "Tuesday, Jan 16." The editor checks his cal-
endar and finds that January 16 is a Wednesday. Did the
writer mean "Wednesday, Jan. 16" or Tuesday, Jan. 15"?

If the editor wants to use the story, he must call the
writer to determine the correct day. If the writer has not
bothered to follow the format suggested in Chapter 2,
the editor will have to look up the telephone number. If
the writer happens to be a woman, she may have given
her name as "Jane Doe" and the telephone directory may
list her number under her husband's name. You can see
how complicated a simple error can become.

Nor is this the end of an editor's responsibility for
the copy before him. In addition to catching errors in

grammar and ensuring the accuracy of information, the editor must deal with stories in other ways.

If an editor feels a story will run longer than its news value warrants, he will trim the piece of any "fat" the writer may have missed. In addition, he may have to cut sentences—or even whole paragraphs—which are redundant.

Often, stories written by non-professionals take on too subjective a tone and the editor must eliminate adjectives to make the story more objective.

Conversely, a non-professional writer may use words which are vague or dull and the editor will substitute more specific or more dynamic words in their place.

Trimming, toning down and making stories crisper through the use of dynamic words all represent tasks which call upon an editor's experience, unlike the "busy work" represented by errors in grammar and spelling.

Still, if too much trimming, toning down or substitution of dynamic words for dull ones is required, the editor may have to rewrite the piece himself or assign it to a reporter to rewrite; that is, if the piece is worth the effort.

If, however, the suggestions in this book are applied, the editor may only have to rewrite a lead, using his experience to construct a first paragraph which will grasp the reader's attention. If the advice in Chapter 6 is followed, the editor may not even have to re-type the lead; he may simply be able to correct its faults with his copy pencil by changing and transposing words.

Another important responsibility of the copy editor is to guard against libel suits. Potentially libelous statements must not be allowed to creep into the paper unnoticed.

Once all these tasks have been performed, the editor determines how the story is to be played; that is, what size and type of headline it will receive and, perhaps, even the page upon which it will appear.

In determining what size headline a story deserves, the editor needs to know if he is dealing with a fresh article or if some previous story has appeared on the same subject in another paper or in his own. An example might be the series stories used to publicize a single project, discussed earlier in this book.

Once the editor has decided upon an appropriate headline, it remains for him to actually write the head.

There is more to headline writing than the layman might imagine. Among other things, the editor must be careful where he breaks off each line of the head in order not to produce what is called a "split" headline; he has to use active words instead of passive ones; he must be aware of what abbreviations he may use and of those he may not; and in every case, he must work within the limits of space prescribed by the number of characters required by the size and style headline he has chosen. It is a time-consuming task.

In the previous ten or fifteen paragraphs, we have discussed many of the considerations which are part of an editor's duties in editing just one story. Multiply that by the many, many stories he must edit in a single day and you begin to appreciate one of the reasons why this book was written. For, if the suggestions presented herein will improve your writing, that improvement will make your local editor's job a great deal easier.

Depending upon the organization of the paper in question, an editor's additional responsibility may be to select photos and prepare them for publication. His duties may include selection and editing stories carried by the wire services. He may have stories or columns of his own to write. On a short-handed staff he may have to retrieve used cuts from the morgue and check old clippings to verify facts. Additionally, it may be he who reads galley proofs and page proofs for errors.

All these activities of the editor are being carried out in the midst of the seemingly constant ringing of telephones, the raucous buzz of police radios, the clatter of typewriters, the metallic clicking of wire machines, discussions with reporters about the accuracy of information, or with printers about points of style, or with other editors about how this story and that should be played. And he is called on to deal with questions from the PTA publicity chairman about newspaper policies, explaining to an irate taxpayer that the newspaper is doing everything within its power to expose waste and corruption in government, and perhaps, even conducting an occasional tour of the newspaper for a local journalism class or some other group. On top of all this is the ever-present pressure of the deadline, which requires that all these activities be carried out by a certain time.

If all this has left you breathless, is it any wonder why editors turn into raving maniacs when they are confronted by poorly prepared news copy?

Years of enduring the transgressions which I have dealt with in this book, and others which I have not, have turned many men into fire-breathing ogres called newspaper editors (and I would imagine that the female of the species is no different). If an editor reads your story and dismisses you with a muffled grunt, consider your job well done.

I have chosen to deal with what my experience has shown are some of the more common failings of nonprofessional publicity chairmen. There is much more that could have been included in these chapters, but the intention was not to try to cram four years of college-level journalism training into a single text.

This book cannot guarantee that your stories will be used on page one, but it may help you to escape from your experience as club publicity chairman with your hair unsinged, your skin unscarred, your hearing intact and more important, better news coverage for your organization.

Glossary

ad—Paid advertisement.

add—The designation given to the second and all subsequent pages of a news or feature story manuscript. The second page of a manuscript is the *first add,* the third page is the *second add,* and so on. Sometimes, pages are numbered "add 1, add 2," etc.

art—Pictures or illustrations used with a story.

banner—A headline consisting of one line of fairly large type which runs across the entire newspaper page.

beat—A specific, continuing assignment, such as a city hall *beat* or police *beat.*

body—The portion of a story exclusive of the lead. In a news story, the body begins with the second paragraph and runs to the end of the story.

box—Lines drawn around a story which give the story more prominent play; also, a story in which the type has been indented from right and left more than the rest of the type on the page.

by-line—A reporter's name at the beginning of a story.

caps—An abbreviation of "capitals," meaning capital letters.

catchline—*See* Slug.

clc—An abbreviation meaning "capitals and lower case."

clean copy—A manuscript which requires little editing and which has few typographical errors.

cold type—A printing process which uses photographic composition.

color story—A feature.

column inch—A unit of measure which is one column wide and one inch deep. *See* Depth.

copyreader—A member of the newspaper staff who edits copy and writes headlines; also called a copyeditor.

credit line—A by-line or a photographer's name used with a
        picture.

crop—The elimination of unwanted or undesirable portions
        of a photograph.

cut—A photoengraving which is used to reproduce a photo-
        graph on the newspaper page.

cutlines—The type which runs beneath a picture, describing
        the action and identifying the subjects.

dateline—A designation placed at the beginning of a story
        which shows the story's place of origin, news
        agency source, and, sometimes, the date.

deadline—The time at which a given newspaper section or
        edition closes and goes to press.

depth—Vertical measurement on a newspaper page.

desk—The section of a newspaper which edits and puts head-
        lines on stories. "Desk" is short for copy desk or city
        desk; a newspaper also may have a sports desk, a
        features desk, a foreign desk, and so on.

down style—A newspaper style which uses capital letters only
        when absolutely necessary. Only proper
        names and capitalized, i.e., Grant school.

dummy—A diagram showing the placement of type, pictures,
        ads and headlines on a newspaper page.

endmark—A symbol, such as "#" or "30," which designates the
        end of a story; the word "end" also may be
        used.

exclusive—A story printed by one and only one newspaper. *See*
        Scoop.

feature—A story which stresses human interest and, unlike the
        news story, one which tries to evoke an emo-
        tional response from the reader.

file—Submitting a story for publication.

fillers—Short items used to fill small spaces in the news col-
        umns.

flag—The paper's nameplate used on page one.

format—The placement on the manuscript page of instruc-
        tional and informational matter which will not be
        printed as part of the story.

galley—A metal tray for holding type.

galley proof—A copy made of type from a galley, upon which corrections are made.

glossy—A photograph printed on shiny paper.

gobbledygook—Language which is difficult to understand.

graph—Short for paragraph.

guideline—*See* Slug.

head—Short for headline.

head and shoulders—The composition preferred for an individual portrait photo; a formal pose which shows only the subject's head and shoulders.

hot metal—A printing process which uses molten metal to cast lines of type, as opposed to a photographic process.

kill—To eliminate unwanted or unnecessary portions of a story, or to eliminate whole stories, pictures or other matter.

label—Often, a headline which contains no verb; a standing head. *See* Wooden Head.

lead—The first paragraph of a news story; the paragraph in which the most significant details of a story are related.

legend—*See* Cutline.

lower case—Small letters, as opposed to capitals.

masthead—Information about the paper which is printed on the editorial page.

mat—Short for matrix paper. Matrix paper is used to make an impression of a finished page and becomes a mold from which the press plate is cast.

morgue—The department of a newspaper in which reference books, clippings and engravings are kept; the paper's library.

newsprint—A low-quality paper.

offset—A photographic printing process.

pad—To make a story longer than it needs to be.

pic—Short for pictures; also written "pix."

play—The prominence with which a story is displayed.

proof—A copy of any printed matter upon which corrections are made.

rim—The position occupied by copy editors on a copy desk.

ROP—An abbreviation for "run of paper." Used to designate less prominent news pages.

scoop—Newspaper slang for an exclusive story, but the connotation usually is that the story involved is a fairly important one.

side bar—An accessory article which is run with a related main story.

slant—The angle or point of view from which a story is written.

slot—The position on a copy desk that is occupied by the chief copy editor or city editor. (Copy desks usually are arranged in a "U" shape and the slot is that position at the mouth of the "U.")

slug—One or two words which are used to identify a story.

split page—The first page of the second section of a newspaper; sometimes called the break page or second front.

squib—A brief news item or filler.

standing head—A headline—often a label—which is kept on hand for repeated use.

streamer—*See* Banner.

stringer—A reporter or correspondent who is not a regular member of the staff; a correspondent who works on a part-time or piecework basis.

style—A body of rules which establishes standard usages for certain grammatical situations or typographical preferences.

take—A portion of a story. Setting a story "in takes" means that portions of a story are sent to the composing room as soon as they are edited, rather than editing an entire story and sending it to the composing room complete.

"30"—Traditionally, the symbol used to mark the end of a story.

tight paper—An edition of a newspaper in which space for news is at a premium.

typo—A typographical error.

underline—*See* Cutline.

up style—A preference for capitalizing words, as opposed to down style.

wooden head—A dull headline.

Index

Accuracy, 102, 108
Active voice, 53–54, 92
"Adds," 16–17
Adjectives. *See* Grammar

Body of news story, 77
Boiling down, 93, 102
Broadening appeal, 42, 96, 99–100, 106,
    119. *See also* Feature story; News
    value

Capitalization, 17, 31, 69–71
Carbon copies, 6–7, 36, 44
Colloquialisms, 76
Comma
    appositives, parenthetical expressions,
        65
    comma splice, 65
    dates, 65
    essential clauses, 65
    names with titles, 66–67
    quoted matter, 61
    series, 66–68
Condensing wordy language, 56–57
Correction materials, 5
Credibility, 102

Dashes, 68
Dateline, 89
Deadlines, 46–47. *See also* "Killing from
        the bottom up"; Lead time
Distribution line, 11–12
Double spacing, 15
Dugan's definition of news, 45

Editorializing, 58
Editors, 48, 151–55
Embargo, 14
Ending a page, 16
Ending a story, 16–17, 126–27

False passive. *See* Grammar

Fasteners, 17
Feature story
    anecdotes, 111, 113–14, 127
    broadening appeal, 107–9, 110–11,
        124–25, 127–28
    compared to news story, 108, 116
    dramatic imagery, 117
    dramatic irony, 125–26
    emotional response, 43, 108, 109, 116,
        118
    ending, 126–27
    "gilding the lily," 118
    human interest, 111, 114–16
    imagination, 108, 111, 113, 116, 117,
        120–22, 122–25, 126, 128
    news triangle modified for, 109–14
    puns, 119–20
    simplicity, 118, 123
    unusual elements in, 120–22, 122–25
    vicarious experience, 116–17
Five W's
    basic building blocks, 79–85
    categories containing more than one
        fact, 85, 95–96
    facts fitting more than one category,
        83–84
    in features, 108, 111, 114–16, 121, 122,
        123
    as organizing tool, 81, 84, 95
    source of positive viewpoint, 90
    in speeches, 100–101, 102
    studying professional stories for, 89
    See also Leads
Flyer style, 68–69
Format, 18, 75, 129–33

Grammar
    adjectives, adverbs, 57, 81
    capitalization, 69–71
    combining ideas, 56–57
    communicating, 52
    difficulties with English, 51–53

false passive, 54–55
passive and active voice, 53–54, 80, 97, 98
prepositions, 56, 81, 88
punctuation, 61–62, 64–68
quotations, 57–62
redundant constructions, 25, 28, 80, 94, 98
simple sentences, 53
spelling, 71, 151
superfluous constructions, 24, 30
third person, 62–63
variety in paragraph beginnings, 88
verb tenses, 63–64

Headlines, 15, 81–82, 106, 153–54
Hyphen, 30, 35, 72

Index cards, 147

Jargon, 76

"Killing from the bottom up," 76–77

Leads
body and, 77
characteristics of good lead, 92–93
delayed in features, 111–12, 115
Five W's as source of, 79, 82, 84, 85, 86, 89, 90, 92, 95, 111
getting to the point, 76
"hooking" the reader, 80, 111, 114, 115–16
improving faults of, 92–98
interrogative, 78–79, 114
negative-positive, 90–92, 114
news lead re-written as a feature, 109–11
"say nothing" leads, 93, 103–4
series stories, 86–88
"shotgun" leads, 85
specificity in, 84, 93, 96, 101, 103–5
from speeches, 100–105
Lead time, 13
Length of stories, 76–77, 123
Letters to the editor, 47, 48

Margins, 15–16
Multiple submissions, 11–12, 44

Newspaper departments, 149–50

News story
declarative approach, 78–79
difficulty of simplicity, 76
lead and body, 77–78
level of language, 75–76
positive viewpoint, 76, 90
purpose of, 78
See also Leads
News value, 40–45, 84, 86, 94, 97, 98. See also Broadening appeal

Objectivity
adjectives, adverbs, 57
direct quotations, 60–61, 87
editorializing, 58
editorial "we," 62
feature story, 107–8, 118
gushing stories, 88, 118
letters to the editor, 47
third person, 58, 62–63

Passive voice. See Grammar
Photoengravings, 137–38
Photographs
composition, 138–45
cost, 137–38
cropping, 139
cutlines, 145–47
desirable proportions, 139–40, 142
news value, 138
policies, 48, 147–48
size and quality, 136–37
"static" posses, 138, 142, 144
Policies
commercial stories, 45
deadlines, 46–47
letters to the editor, 47
lists of names, 67–68
multiple submissions, 44
pictures, 48, 147–48
public service stories, 45
series stories, 88
telephone numbers, 45–46
value of space, 43–44
where to look for statement of, in newspaper, 38–40
See also Taboos
Positive viewpoint, 90, 92
Prepositions. See Grammar
Proofreaders' marks, 5

Quotations, 57–61, 61–62, 87–88, 93

Release date, 12–14
Redundant constructions. *See* Grammar

Semicolon, 65–68
Series stories, 7, 42, 86–88, 143–44
Simplicity, 52, 68–69, 76, 118, 123
Slash, 35
Slugging stories, 10–11, 15, 16
Sources of stories
    features from news, 109–11
    meetings, 97–98
    negative events, 90
    nose for news, 89
    organization events, 80, 82–85, 96–97,
        110, 113–14, 119–20
    recognizing hidden elements, 99,
        120–25
    series from single event, 86
    services and programs, 100, 115–17,
        125–26, 127–28
    speeches, 94, 100–105
    See also Five W's; Leads
Spelling, 71
Standing headlines, 81–82
Statistical material, 92–93, 101, 102
Style
    abbreviations, 20, 22, 25, 27, 28, 30,
        31–32
    cutlines, 145–47
    dates and times, 22–25
    decimals, 33
    editing for, 7
    fractions, 35

literary style in feature story, 108
    in literature, 19–20
    matter of preference, 21
    military titles, 30–31
    monetary figures, 34
    names of people, 26
    numbers, 32–33
    official titles, 29–30
    over-and-under-10 rule for numbers,
        33–35
    percentages, 34
    polite address, 25–27, 95
    professional titles, 27–29, 95
    titles for clergymen, 28–29
    women's liberation, use of Ms., 26
Stylebook, 20–22, 49

Taboos
    carbon copies, 44
    headlines, 15
    leads for features, 114
    multiple submissions, 11, 43, 44
    staples, 17
    typing, 15, 17
Time reference, 86–87
Triangular structure of stories, 77, 81,
        102, 107, 109–14
Type cleaner, 4
Typewriter, 1–4
Typing paper, 4–5

Verbs
    as "what" elements in leads, 82
    present perfect tense, 63–64

_ADW4837